With Dad
ON A
Deer Stand

Unforgettable Stories of
Adventure in the Woods

Steve Chapman

AUTHOR OF *A Look at Life from a Deer Stand*

HARVEST HOUSE PUBLISHERS
EUGENE, OREGON

WITH DAD ON A DEER STAND
Copyright © 2013 by Steve Chapman
Published by Harvest House Publishers
Eugene, Oregon 97402
www.harvesthousepublishers.com

Library of Congress Cataloging-in-Publication Data
Chapman, Steve.
  With dad on a deer stand / Steve Chapman.
    pages cm
  ISBN 978-0-7369-5312-2 (pbk.)
  ISBN 978-0-7369-5313-9 (eBook)
  1. Hunting—Religious aspects—Christianity. 2. Deer hunting—Anecdotes. 3. Father and child—Religious aspects—Christianity. I. Title.
  BV4597.4.C44 2013
  242'.68—dc23

                                                                2012047385

Printed in the United States of America

          13 14 15 16 17 18 19 20 / BP-JH / 10 9 8 7 6 5 4 3 2 1

I'd like to extend special thanks to...

Nathan and *Heidi,* my two children, for allowing me to tell some of their stories. What awesome gifts they are to my life.

George Ferrell, my cousin in West Virginia, for his willingness to share his stories about hunting with his dad (my late Uncle Jimmy Ferrell). We all look forward to seeing him again when we get to the camper in heaven.

Lindsey Williams, father of two, for his friendship and for being an example of a great dad.

Chuck Weaver for the use of his dad's words in the story "Nothing Like the Last One."

Acknowledgments

I'd like to thank these contributors for letting me include their stories.

Charles J. Alsheimer, father of one from New York; outdoor writer and photographer; www.CharlesAlsheimer.com.

Alice Click, mother of two from West Virginia (and Annie's sister); editor for Today's Conservative Women of West Virginia; Daughters of the American Revolution historian.

Jason Cruise, father of two from Tennessee; author, speaker, and video producer in the hunting industry; founder of MISSION, www.TheMission Vision.net; www.JasonCruiseSpeaks.com.

Dan Field, father of two from Illinois; founder of ProVision Productions, www.provisionproductions.net.

Chad Gilliland, father of two from Oregon; industrial engineer.

Brad Herndon, father of three (one in heaven) from Indiana; freelance outdoor writer and photographer.

Paul Meeks, father of four from Louisiana; owner and president of Great Day, Inc.

Randy Petrich, father of three from Montana; rancher and outfitter; owner of Rising Son Outfitters, www.huntinginmontana.com.

Tim Smith, father of one from Alabama; founder of On Target Outdoor Ministries, www.ontargetoutdoorministries.com; co-owner of On Target Media.

Dan Swartz, father of two from Ohio; product support manager at Ventrac-Venture Products, Inc., www.ventrac.com; cofounder of Lasting Flame Marriage Seminar, www.lastingflame.org.

Brodie Swisher, father of four in Montana; www.realitybowhunting.com.

Paul Walerczak, father of seven from Indiana; founder of Without Excuse Ministries, www.withoutexcuseministries.com; executive producer of Without Excuse Ministries videos; public speaker; Fortune Brands Home and Security distributor; corporate pilot.

Contents

A Special Legacy

I got a call from a gentleman named Randy Reese some years ago. He sounded like he was nearly in tears as he told me about his father dying and what was found when the family went through his dad's things. It was a copy of one of my hardbound gift books titled *Pursuing the Prize*. What made this even more special was that his dad had handwritten the thoughts of his heart on the inside cover pages. These were things he'd never shared with his family. Randy was overwhelmed with joy to find such a treasure. With his permission, I'm sharing with you some of what his dad wrote:

> Thanks be to God my Creator, my father, and my brother for taking me [hunting] and putting up with me as a youngster full of questions. I am thankful for each sunrise and sunset I have witnessed in the outdoors. I feel at home with God each time I occupy His great outdoors.
>
> My preacher once made it perfectly clear that my prayers on a deer stand would be interrupted by gunfire should I hear the sound of [hooves] in the leaves. I have been fortunate in my life to have had many, many opportunities to spend countless hours, days, months, and years in a treestand.
>
> I am thankful to God for the opportunity to raise my sons

in God's creation, with the clear understanding that hunting is in our blood, and it is not about the kill but the thrill that drives us. I cannot tell you the number of times my sons and I, after a harvest of an animal, have placed our hands on the animal and prayed to God [about] the opportunity not just to hunt an animal but to share the experience of being together…

I have learned two things through my ventures in the outdoors. In order to grow as a hunter, you have to spend countless hours on a stand or in the woods to become a true woodsman. I have also, through this same set of circumstances, learned that to truly grow as a Christian it takes time. Years of studying, patience, failure, and success to grow in the Lord.

I pray my sons continue to learn that hunting is a learning experience. It is a time alone in the woods to study God's creation, as well as a time to grow closer to the Creator. Let each failed hunt teach you a lesson as well as each failed Christian experience teach you the correct way to walk with God. Read His Word. Study as if trying to figure the ways of a mature whitetail, and you will grow in the Lord.

Thank You, my dear precious God, for each experience with my sons in your outdoors, as well as the many prayers we shared in the woods together with tears in our eyes. Those experiences were the harvest.

Grow, my children, as well as my wife, whom I love unconditionally. Without her I could not be me. In Your Word or in whatever way You choose to bring them closer to You, thank You, Jesus, for Your answers to my prayers. Thank You, thank You.

Some folks have Oscars on their shelves, some have Tony or Emmy Awards, and others have major sports trophies to show. I'm sure they're nice to have, but as far as I'm concerned, Mr. Reese's handwritten letter to his sons in one of my books rivals all the hardware that has ever been handed out at award shows. What an honor to have been a small part of such a valuable heirloom for the Reese family. I'm confident this dad's intention was to personally hand the book to his boys at some point, and that he never expected his passing would prevent it. I'm also quite sure that when his grieving sons read their dad's words, they were made doubly meaningful in light of the sadness of his absence.

As I imagined the look on their faces when their eyes took in the written thoughts of their father and favorite hunting companion, I began to think of other dad/child relationships that have been made better and stronger by their mutual enjoyment of hunting. With that in mind, it seemed good to gather some stories about dads hunting with their children, as well as kids hunting with their fathers. The purpose is twofold: to share some unforgettable adventures with you and to inspire you to keep going to the woods and fields with your family members to create wonderful, lifelong memories.

The book you hold in your hand contains accounts from the memory banks of some good friends who are great dads, one pro-hunting mom, some stories from my time in the woods with my kids, as well as a few adventures I've written based on real-life experiences and circumstances I've heard about while spending time with hunters. If any of them stir you to write down the treasure of your words to your kids, you're welcome to use the inside pages of this book as your writing pad. I'd be honored.

Happy and safe hunting to you and yours,

Steve Chapman

1

Making Somethin' Happen

by Steve Chapman

There is a saying that a lot of turkey hunters use when the springtime gobblers are being way too quiet, thus making hunting slow and laborious: "If they ain't talkin', I'm walkin'!" These words are normally muttered with a bit of exasperation and are typically said about a microsecond after the derriere announces that it can't endure sitting on the hard ground any longer.

Usually before this statement is completed, the packing-up process starts. After gathering up the slate calls, strikers, and box calls that were laid out on the ground within easy reach and putting them back in their designated pockets in a waist pack, the eager turkey hunter stands and is on his way to either check out some fields or walk around to do some contact calling.

How do I know so much about the tendency of a turkey hunter to be so impulsive? Simply because I am among their number. More than once I've whispered those words of frustration to myself or to a friend, and within a minute or two the hunting party is on the move.

Deer hunters can be just as impetuous, and I'm numbered among them as well. I've been known to mumble, "If they ain't gruntin', I'm goin' huntin'!" These code words for "If I sit here any longer I'm gonna freeze to death" have been used in the past to get me moving. My standard reaction to a hunt that has gone bland is to exclaim, "It's time to make somethin' happen!" It would be embarrassing to admit how many times that slightly irritated declaration has resulted in my quick descent out of a treestand. Yes, I have a tendency to succumb to impatience, and it's definitely something I need to work on. But every once in a great while, my "get up and go" yields something good. Such was the case for a deer hunt my son and I enjoyed several years ago.

Nathan was home from college for a Thanksgiving visit. Due to his heavy study schedule, he'd warned us that he could stay only from Wednesday to Saturday morning. That year Tennessee's firearm deer season was scheduled to start Thanksgiving Day. Though I wanted to go to a nearby farm for a hunt that morning, I did the smart thing and conceded to my wife's wishes that everyone be home when the big noontime meal was served. Consequently, I assumed that with Nathan's short stay we wouldn't get to the woods at all. I quietly but reluctantly resolved myself to that likelihood.

When Friday afternoon arrived, my hopes were resurrected. Nathan approached and asked the question I'd hoped to hear.

"Dad, do you think we could go hunting tomorrow morning before I drive back to school?"

Bingo! "You bet, buddy," I quickly replied. "We can go to Joe's place. I'll put you in the ladder stand at the edge of a soybean field. There's plenty of deer, and there are lots of residual beans on the ground to attract them. With the hunting license you have, you can take either a buck or a doe, so you should be able to fill your tag. We'll go before daylight in the morning. If things go well, you should be on the road back to school by 10 o'clock."

Dawn came Saturday morning with Nathan on one end of the 180-acre farm perched in an 18-foot-high, metal ladder stand. The stand's placement was next to a thicket where deer loved to bed down during the day. I was sitting on a stool at the other end of the property next to a harvested cornfield. I waited for the deer to appear and hoped to hear the report of Nathan's .270. But there were no blasts to be heard. Eventually I was concerned, worried that my son wouldn't get an opportunity to take a shot. After another 15 minutes of wishful listening, words tumbled out of my mouth. I seemed to have no more control over them than I have over an avalanche on a Colorado mountainside. "It's time to make somethin' happen!"

With that said, I promptly stood up, folded my three-legged stool and tucked it under my arm, shouldered my rifle, and headed to the north side of the farm. When I got to the ladder stand, it was around nine. I looked up at Nathan and asked the obvious question. "See anything at all, Nate?"

His reply was gracious. "No deer, Dad. Just a beautiful sunrise, a few blue jays, and a couple of squirrels. But it's been a great morning. I guess we'd better go to the house so I can get ready to head back to school."

While I sensed his sincere gratitude for the chance to be in a deer stand at least one morning that year, I also detected a bit of disappointment. Feeling some fatherly sorrow for the boy, I offered an opportunity I was sure he'd agree to. "Nate," I whispered as softly as I could, "it's time to make somethin' happen."

There were those words again! This wasn't the first time Nathan had heard me say them while deer hunting. Through the years during hunts, he'd been on the receiving end of several "deer drives" that started with my "Let's make somethin' happen!" exclamation. When I did resort to this tactic, I was always careful and quick to remind him, "Son, this isn't always the best way to hunt, but sometimes you just have to stir 'em up to see some action." I had no idea that I was teaching him a principle that would serve him well later on in life.

Nathan knew exactly what I meant by making something happen, and he smiled down at me as I continued. "How about you stay put for about 15 minutes while I walk down this fencerow and get into the thicket behind you. Since its nine o'clock, some deer may have come in from the other side and bedded down. If there's something in there, maybe I'll push it out and you might get a shot."

"Yeah, I'd be happy to stay here," Nathan replied.

I took off. When I got about 200 yards down the fence line, I took a hard right. It took me a few minutes to loop around, but I stepped into the thicket and started pressing through the heavy brush and briars toward Nathan's position. When I got about a 100 yards from where he was sitting, I heard the sweet sound of his .270 announcing that I had indeed stirred up a bedding deer. I couldn't have been happier. Three more booms in quick succession occurred as I stood in the middle of the thicket. I had an experienced guess at what was happening, so I added a running commentary as the shots sounded.

Bang! "Oh, yes!"

Bang! "Oh, wow!"

Bang! "Oh no!"

Bang! "Oh well…"

As quickly as I could get through the thorns that clawed viciously at my camo, I returned to the ladder stand where my son waited. He was standing on the ground, and he reloaded as we talked.

"Do you think you got one, Nate?"

"Nah. I don't think I touched him. He was a big-bodied deer, Dad. Nice rack too. I could see the dust flying up around him as I shot, so no, I don't think I touched him."

"Well, we won't leave the farm until we've made sure he's not hurt," I responded.

Then I heard my son say something that has been etched in my mind since that moment. It's a confession we've both laughed about for years in the retelling.

"Dad, I need to tell you something."

"What is it, son?" I was ready for anything from "I think I shot my toe off" to "I'm gonna drop out of college and join the circus." Instead, it was something much more grave.

"Dad, when I took that last shot, I could see your truck in the scope."

I know my face turned pale when I heard his humble admission. I looked toward the truck and immediately tried to give my son the benefit of the doubt.

"That's an awfully long way for a bullet to travel, buddy. But if the old pickup is dead, we'll get it mounted and hang it over the mantel."

We spent the next hour looking for signs of a bleeding deer but found none. When we got to the truck, we checked it over and didn't find any bullet holes in it either. Since it started up right away, we headed home. Nathan did his best to assure me he'd had a great morning even though his tag would go unpunched for the year. I accepted his assessment of the day, and we stored the memory away to enjoy in the years to come.

When he was out of college and married, I discovered my son had found something redeemable in my "It's time to make somethin' happen" attitude that he'd seen and experienced while hunting with me. The advice I'd given him that it wasn't the best way to go about deer hunting was well-received, but so was the other part of my instruction. He'd accepted the reality that sometimes it is necessary to "stir things up." He realized the tactic wasn't just valuable in the woods, but that it could also be effective in the business world. And apply it he did!

Being a musician by trade, I bought Nathan an electric/acoustic guitar as a Christmas gift when he was 10 years old. When he opened it, I told him, "Son, your job is to not just learn how to play that guitar, but I want you to learn how to make it talk!" Never did a youngster take a dad's challenge more seriously. He proceeded to spend untold hours learning scales, discovering how to read music charts, and trying to mimic great players, such as Phil Keaggy, Stevie Ray Vaughn, Eric Johnson, and Eric Clapton.

As he was learning to play the guitar, I also passed down some old recording equipment we'd used in our family business of writing songs, recording music, and putting on concerts. When we replaced a recording machine with the latest technology, Nate got the earlier version. Within a short time, he was skilled on the guitar and was developing an in-depth understanding of "signal path" (meaning he was learning how to be a recording engineer). Nathan's skills as a musician and engineer eventually became good enough to enlist him in updating some of the earlier recordings my wife, Annie, and I had released.

After marrying Stephanie, Nathan worked a few jobs that included being a cashier at a bookstore and roofing, but music was his first love when it came to doing something that would earn a wage. He considered entering the business of music by performing, but he wasn't that fond of being center stage. After "sitting on the music stand" for a while and seeing nothing really generate with his musical skills, he decided, "It's time to make somethin' happen!"

Armed with a stack of CDs containing samples of his ability to produce full-blown studio versions of songs featuring his guitar, his bass, his keyboard, his drums, and his engineering prowess, he hit the streets of Nashville. Willing to face rejection, he marched into the offices of publishers on Music Row, handed them a disc, and said something akin to "I can do your songwriter demos fast and cheap, and they'll sound good. Give me a chance, and I'll prove it to you!"

When publishers hear "fast, cheap, and will sound good," that's music to their ears! As a result of his brave presentations, he landed opportunities to make some music as well as get some dollars going his way. Then one day, the big payoff came for his "make somethin' happen" efforts. An established songwriter Nathan had worked with brought in a 15-year-old songwriter to collaborate with. Nathan heard something in their co-writes that made him perk up. He offered to produce a couple of songs for the two writers on a gratis basis, quietly hoping they'd let him continue as their go-to guy for song demos.

The music Nathan produced for that 15-year-old songwriter got the attention of the team that surrounded her, and they hired him to work with her on a full CD. Her initial recordings were very well received by country music radio networks and yielded a couple "top of the chart" singles. On the heels of that success work, they began work on a second CD. The follow-up recording generated so much commercial success that it was nominated for and won a Grammy Award for album of the year, the music world's equivalent of the Super Bowl, Daytona 500, or World Series.

Nathan has worked with other recognizable artists I could mention, but suffice it to say that he remains plenty busy as a producer as well as a songwriter. Each time I hear his handiwork on the radio or TV, I marvel at what he's accomplished. I'm proud of how his solid work ethic has served him well in the world of music, but I'm even more excited when I hear Nate give God thanks for everything he's achieved.

As I bask in the glowing joy of a son whose industrious spirit has yielded such accomplishments, I also wonder where he'd be today if he hadn't been willing to respond to the urge to get up and hit the streets of Nashville. I know I can't take total credit for his relentless fortitude, but I like to think that just maybe a few of those "let's make somethin' happen" moments we had while deer hunting helped shape his drive for success.

2

Obsessions and Sunrises

by Jason Cruise

The Marlin .30-30 was about the same size as I was when I started hunting Ms. Stone's farm with my dad. He had master-crafted two identical ladder stands out of pine planks that would be, literally and figuratively, the foundation upon which my journey with the whitetail would begin. I introduced my first 21 whitetails to the sound of that gun's hammer dropping and my beating heart at that farm. In the first few years, Dad hung those stands about 150 yards apart in a white oak flat that allowed me just enough freedom to feel like I was entering manhood while, at the same time, offering Dad just enough space that he knew he could get to me in about two minutes if he felt the need. As the years grew, the distance between our stands did the same.

I don't have a solid ability for memory recall of my childhood years, and I can't understand why. My childhood was filled with as much love as a kid could ask for, so it doesn't make sense why my memories are foggy. I do, however, recall with high-definition the serendipity that occurred one November morning at the Stone farm. Dad asked me a question that would forever alter my tenacious pursuit of trophy whitetails.

I was in my teens when the question came. I've heard many men describe their sons as "15 going on 30." By my best guess I was 15 going on arrogant. This particular morning was honestly about as Norman Rockwell as whitetail hunting can be. There was frost on the ground an inch thick that reflected the orange hues of a sunrise in a cloudless sky.

Dad was hunting a stand we'd hung where a large bean field gave way to a deer bedding area. I was in my traditional spot on the southeast side of the farm, sitting with my spine tight to the maple tree that housed the same ladder stand I'd hunted on from day one. This stand location was nothing short of a killing tree. Perched perfectly on a small rise, it was a pinch-point where whitetails cruised their way from the bean field where Dad was sitting to some very old white oaks that provided the acorns that were always the deer's last meal of the morning as they made their way to a midday bedding area.

Not much happened this particular morning, and with my appetite feeling the mounting pressure of the thought of hot food, my boots hit the ground and I was off to catch up with Dad. Having not heard a shot from his general direction, I figured his hunt had gone about the same as mine. I didn't feel too much remorse about coming down at nine o'clock to head for breakfast.

We'd decided to meet at a worn-down crossing where the creek flattened out, which made it normally a very shallow flow of water. This year it was dry altogether. As I rounded a bend in the logging road, there was Dad standing by a fencepost. He was looking off into the distance at nothing in particular, as far as I could tell. Evidently he'd given up even sooner than I had. My first question was the same one I'd asked him many times before. It was the only question I thought worth asking any hunter serious about his endeavors.

"See anything?"

"A few. Nothing special," he replied.

Then came the words that haunt me to this day.

"Did you see the sunrise, son? My, my, it was beautiful."

I was a bit thrown off my game, to tell you the truth. My inner voice immediately spoke up. *No, I didn't see the sunrise. Of course I didn't watch the sun go up. I was too busy watching for any movement of a deer sneaking its way through that oak flat. I'm guessing the reason you saw "nothing special" was because you were too busy watching the sky.*

That was my inner voice which, thankfully, never made its way to my actual voice. That would have surely landed me within some form of well-deserved grip on my collarbone causing me to bow in submission. Instead, all I said was, "No, I didn't see it."

Dad shouldered his gun sling. As he started to walk off with me, he said simply, "Always watch the sunrise, son. There's more to it than what you see."

At the time I had no idea that hunting would become more than a hobby. Now that I've spent the last ten years or so writing, speaking, and filming within the hunting industry, I can personally attest to damages caused by unbridled obsessions with trophy whitetails. Unfortunately, I've lived some of them out. For example, fixations on mounting numbers for a trophy room can cause a hunter to miss the best moments that a trip to the wild can offer.

One such moment came just a few seasons ago when I took my eldest son, Cole, on a turkey hunt. Having seen a mature strutter in a field, we decided to make a mad dash to get to him in hopes of getting a shot. There was only one problem in my immediate future, and I knew it before ever getting out of the truck. We were going to have to cross a shallow creek. I wasn't worried about the camera gear or even getting Cole across the water. He was tall enough for sure. I was worried about the fact that I knew this bird wasn't going to hang out in the field forever. I also knew full well that five-year-old Cole wasn't about to cross such a picturesque creek without slam-dunking a few rocks.

And that posed two problems. One was the noise of him hurling stones into water like a Celtic warrior in training for battle. The other was the time it was going to take to fulfill his extreme obsession with rock throwing. Sure enough, we got to the creek and he said, "Dad, can I throw some rocks in that water?" With a smile on my face and a grimace in my heart, I said, "Sure, bud. Have at it."

A few minutes passed, and he was ready to go. I was too. I was ready to go to the truck because I was sure that turkey had heard every clamoring clang of those rocks. But being the diehard gobbler-getter that I am, I felt compelled to finish the sneak. We climbed up the creek bank and made our way to the pasture, about 120 yards away.

Cole was running the camera because he was too small to hold up a gun. I let out a string of turkey yelps with my mouth call, and that tom hammered down hard with a reply. Seven minutes later we were filming post-kill segments to wrap up some world-class footage of a strutter working his way through a grass field. It's the kind of video only an April morning hunt can provide for the heart of a hunter.

I've heard it said that creation was God's first missionary. I believe that statement with all my heart. The Scriptures testify to the truth of creation's witness: "Since the creation of the world [God's] invisible attributes, His eternal power and divine nature, have been clearly seen, being understood through what has been made, so that [people] are without excuse" (Romans 1:20 NASB).

Sometimes I wonder if the willingness and ability to slow down and appreciate *every* aspect of hunting instead of just punching a tag somehow skipped a generation and landed on Cole. He was quick to thank God for the thrill of the kill and mentioned what a beautiful farm we were privileged to be hunting on. I was humbled. It seems that no matter how old I am or whether I'm chasing whitetails or toms, God has forever graced me with a man or a man-in-the-making in my life who holds me accountable to recognize the glory of our great God through His creation. I'm glad the "grateful gene" is still growing on the family tree.

3

That's What Boys Do

by Brodie Swisher

Children are a gift from God, no doubt. But when those little guys are born during hunting season, a dad's time in the deer woods can quickly get tossed to the back of the truck as more important priorities find their places. Such was the case when I dove headfirst into the world of being a daddy. I have three kids on this earth, and they were all born smack in the middle of hunting season. My wife refers to it as perfect and precious. I call it poor planning.

My daughter, Avery, was born on August 15, also known as opening day of archery antelope in our home state of Montana. My two boys, Aidan and Easton, were born the last week of October, although in different years. Their birthdays always coincide with the opening weekend of rifle season for deer. There was only one solution to this annual dilemma of negligence in the deer woods. I would begin the tradition of my boys celebrating their birthday with dad in the woods! So when my son Aidan turned three, I decided it was time to begin our annual mantime adventure.

I decided highlights of our times together would always include looking for critters to slay, riding in the truck, eating cold sausage, biscuits, and donuts chased down with chocolate milk. There would also be plenty of rock chunkin', tinklin' in the woods, and a long list of other activities that boys should do with their dads. From time to time, Aidan would ask why we did the things we did on those man-time moments when we were free of girls. I always offered him this simple fact: "That's what boys do."

Over the years, our hunts continued to evolve with each passing hunting season. That first season we drove up on the mountain and simply glassed the opposite hillsides for any signs of the critters we pursued. The next year I packed Aidan in my backpack, and we hit the trail. He got the easy part by riding on my back. The fact that we always seemed to scare off more wildlife than we encountered never seemed to be a deal-breaker for him. He was perfectly content to be along on a hunt with his dad. And, as little guys often do, he asked questions nonstop.

"Why do we eat sunflower seeds?"

"Why do we belch and burp?"

"Why did you try to run over Mrs. Andrews' cat?"

"Why do we get to go potty anywhere we want?"

The answer I typically gave stayed the same: "That's just what boys do." On the fourth year of our annual pilgrimage to the deer woods on Aidan's birthday, I realized he was starting to get the picture of "what boys do."

It was a cold morning in late October when Aidan's sixth birthday rolled around. Well before daylight, I snuck into his room and, like a forklift, lifted Aidan from the top bunk while trying my best not to wake his little brother. We made our way down to the man cave. We each had our pile of camo gear ready to go. Aidan was proud of having his own "hunting stuff." He'd even talked his mom into buying him a camo backpack. He was quickly learning that collecting hunting gear and camo duds was definitely something boys do.

The temperature outside was below freezing, and deer pre-rut activity was in full swing. On birthday hunts, any legal critter was considered pursuable. While we'd encountered a variety of game over the years on Aidan's special day, we had yet to punch a tag. We had high hopes that this year would be different.

After we arrived at the farm where we were going to hunt, we made the trek from the truck to the ground blind as quickly as we could. The break of day was obviously on its way. We unloaded our abundance of gear in the blind and then climbed in. I'd packed a small propane heater on this hunt in an effort to keep little Aidan warm despite the outside temperature holding steady around the 20-degree mark. The warm glow of the heater brought warmth to our fingers and a smile to Aidan's face as we settled in for our morning sit. Fortunately for us, we didn't wait long before the action happened.

As the sun poked its brilliant face over the mountain, I caught movement coming from the upper field. A quick look with the binoculars revealed a nice group of mature does making their way from feeding in the field to bedding down in the timber. They were on a trail that would lead right past our blind. Aidan and I went into the nervous scramble that precedes most encounters with wild game within bow range. I placed the camera and tripod in front of Aidan so he could do his best to capture whatever would take place.

Without a clue we were in the world, the does made their way right up in front of our blind. I was already at full draw when little Aidan excitedly whispered, "Shoot her!"

In a flash, the arrow was gone. The shot looked and felt good. Aidan jumped up out of his seat. We celebrated our success with hugs, high-fives, and knuckle butts.

"I knew you could do it, Dad!" Aidan shouted. "That's how we do it!"

I'd enjoyed bonding previously with my little boy through our adventures in the field, but this day was different. We'd shed blood together in the deer woods. We spent a few priceless moments in the ground blind talking through what had just happened. It was a conversation about an experience that seemed to latch our hearts together like little else could.

As we talked, the look on Aidan's face told me that the excitement was more than one little guy could possibly stand. As I collected our gear and prepared to go put a tag on our prize, Aidan was answering the call of nature. When I heard the familiar sound, I looked back at my son who was standing in the corner of our ground blind. In the excitement, he was tinkling all over my backpack! With a post-tinkle shiver and a smile from ear to ear, he said, "That's what boys do!"

As we walked out of the field that day towing our deer, Aidan made a comment I've remembered to this day.

"I had the best time with you today, Daddy!"

It's hard to explain how good those words sounded to me. I want to be remembered by my boys as a dad who taught them more than simply what it means to be a boy. I want to teach them what it means to be a man. And not just a good man—but a godly man. As we journey together, I want them to see Christ in and through me all along the way. When I hear my boys say, "I want to be like Dad!" I want to know that it means they also desire to be like Christ.

I love the assurance found in Proverbs 22:6: "Train up a child in the way he should go, even when he is old he will not depart from it" (NASB).

4

The Call

by Steve Chapman

Danny picked up the phone and pushed 4 of the 11 digits of his dad's long-distance number. Then he stopped. He paused to think again about what he was about to do. After five seconds or so, he pressed the off button and whispered, "What if he says no?"

Chasing whitetails was a passion that had not been handed down to him from his father, who had never shown any interest in it. For that reason, Danny was well aware that his dad's response to his proposal could go either way. Hoping to say just the right words to entice him, Danny had rehearsed the invitation many times. As he held the phone and debated whether or not to complete the call, he went over the idea one more time.

> *Hey, Dad, a few of my buddies and I are headed to the mountains in a couple of weeks for opening day of rifle season. I wanted to call to see if you'd like to go along. We have plenty of room in the cabin for you. I'll treat you and provide a rifle, ammunition, a buck tag, and all the warm clothes you'll need. And there'll be lots of good food there—enough to feed an army. You won't need to bring a thing but your plans for a good time with us. It'll be more fun than you can imagine. Wanna go?*

Feeling hopeful that he would remember every word, Danny dug for courage, pushed all 11 buttons of his dad's phone number and waited anxiously for his dad to answer.

"Hello."

"Hey, Dad. Danny here. Wanna go deer huntin' with us on opening day in a couple of weeks?" The combination of intensely wishing that his dream of hearing "yes" from his dad would come true and the terrible dread of hearing "no" instead had wiped Danny's memory clean of his rehearsed words. He couldn't believe how he'd mentally locked up at the crucial moment. The dead silence on the other end of the line was painful to hear. Without the extra enticements of food, a free license, and fun, Danny was sure the long pause would be followed by, "Naw, son, I don't think I want to do that. Hope you have a great time though. Thank you for asking." Then the real answer came.

"You know, son, I've been thinking about going with you to see what it is about this huntin' thing that you like so much. I don't know the first thing about deer hunting, but if you're willing to take a greenhorn along with you, I'm game."

Danny couldn't believe his ears! He was glad his dad couldn't see him do four strong victory pumps with his fist and then look up to heaven and quietly mouth, *Thank You, God! You heard and answered my prayer!*

"Son, other than a good pair of boots, I don't have any of the gear I'll need, so I'll have to borrow some of that camo stuff from you, as well as use one of your rifles, if that's okay. You'll also have to show me how to shoot."

Danny smiled big as he spoke. "I can definitely show you how to use my .30-06. And I have everything you'll need when it comes to warm camo clothes. And by the way, after we hang up I'm going to the store to get your deer license. My treat—and I insist." He'd finally remembered the rest of his rehearsed invitation, so he added an enhanced version of it. "There's plenty of room in the cabin for you, my buddies and I will supply all the food, and best of all, you're gonna enjoy the guys we'll be with. They're all first-class, very safety conscious, and we'll make sure you get a good spot on the property in terms of where the deer are."

"Thanks, son. You certainly don't have to get my license for me, but I can tell by the tone of your voice that I probably can't change your mind about that. I'll meet you at your house in two weeks. If it's all right with you and Sherrie, I'll bring your mama with me so she can visit with Sherrie and help out with the kids while we're gone. A young mom can always use a break, and your mama is itching for some grandbaby time."

Danny said that was a good plan and thanked his dad for agreeing to come for the trip. After saying good-bye and replacing the phone's handset in the cradle, he turned and went dancing through his house like a little boy who'd just found out he was going to a Major League baseball game.

The next 14 days passed way too slow, but Danny busied himself by getting things ready for the first-ever hunting trip to the mountains with his dad.

The day finally came when his dad and mom arrived. After settling his mom in and transferring his dad's gear to his rig, Danny announced it was time to head out. After the good-byes, Danny and his dad had a good visit as they headed into the mountains. When they rounded the last curve in the dirt road that brought the log cabin into view, Danny's heart was pounding with excitement. The rustic setting looked like a picture in a magazine.

"Whoa!" was all his dad could say as the truck came to a stop and he took in the view. "This place looks incredible! I saw the pictures you sent, of course, but I had no idea how great it would look live. And you were involved in building this cabin? I'm amazed."

Danny's chest swelled a little. "I sure was. My three hunting buddies and I built this place. Don't forget, among the four of us, one is a contractor and one is an electrician. Even though I push a pencil, I learn quickly. I was able to do a lot of nail pounding, some roofing, and even remembered some of the stuff you taught me about plumbing. I was glad I could contribute. It was pure fun to build this place."

As the two of them sat in the cab of the truck admiring the cabin and surrounding country, the other hunters pulled up in separate trucks. Everyone piled out and introductions were done.

"Hey, guys, this is my dad, Jerry," Danny announced. "Dad, this is Tom, Brandon, and Gregg." After a network of handshakes and a few minutes of friendly chitchat, the unloading process began. Within 30 minutes the men had settled in and were enjoying the warm flames in the woodstove.

Feeling anxious to introduce his dad to the bolt-action .30-06 he'd be using, Danny stood up and spoke. "Hey, guys, I'm gonna take Dad outside and let him get acquainted with my Remington. I'm also going to sight-in my .308 to make sure it's dead on. Anybody else need to double-check his weapon?"

All five hunters grabbed their gun cases and headed to the 100-yard shooting lane that had been cleared in the area behind the cabin. It took only a couple of shots each for Danny, Tom, Brandon, and Gregg to feel satisfied their guns were sighted in. Within a few minutes it was Jerry's turn to take his place at the homemade shooting table. He seemed a little nervous as Danny showed him how to work the safety.

Jerry noticed how confidently his boy pushed a fully loaded clip into the underside of the rifle and explained the basics of how the gun operated.

"Have a seat here, Dad. Rest the barrel on the sandbags and look through the scope. Do you see the familiar sight of the crosshairs?"

Jerry nodded.

"Great. Look down the lane at the paper target. Tell me if everything looks in focus."

"Looks good to me, son. Looks just like the pictures I've seen of looking through scopes at targets. What now?"

Danny again showed his dad how to use the bolt action.

Jerry followed the instructions, and the metallic sound and feel of the cartridge being transferred from the clip into the chamber caught his attention. "Yeah! That sounds rather manly!" he exclaimed.

Danny looked at his friends and grinned. "Cool, isn't it, Dad. Now, to fire this rifle, you make sure the butt is snug against your shoulder, slide the safety button forward, put the crosshairs on the big orange dot on the target, and slowly pull the trigger. The gun will kick back into your shoulder a little as it fires, but nothing you can't handle."

After a few moments of settling in on the target, Jerry pulled the trigger and felt the sudden jolt of the gun against his shoulder. Stunned, he sat silently for about three seconds. He looked up, turned to the guys, focused on Danny, and gave his post-shot report. "I thought the sound of the bolt action was manly, but that was nothing compared to pulling the trigger! That's what I call a big-time testosterone moment! But how'd I do? Did I hit the target?"

All three of Danny's friends looked through their binoculars and almost simultaneously said, "Dead deer, Mr. Jerry!"

"You can look through the scope and see where it hit, Dad," Danny encouraged with a wide smile.

Jerry put his eye to the scope and saw that the bullet mark was on the right edge of the two-inch orange dot.

"May I shoot some more?" Jerry's voice revealed his excitement. He wanted to get back to the fun.

"Absolutely, Dad. In fact, I have two boxes of shells for you. You can take 39 more shots if you want. But since it's starting to get dark, I think 5 or 10 more shots will give you the skill you need to be ready to hunt tomorrow."

With the sighting-in process done and a meal of hot pizza under their belts, the five hunters bedded down for the night.

Jerry smiled in the dark as he listened to the group strategize about the next morning. As they talked back and forth, he could hear their excitement. While they were still making their plans, he drifted off to sleep.

It didn't seem but a minute of sleep to all of them when the alarm buzzer woke them the next morning. Following some cereal and coffee, the camo-clad crew headed to the porch to cover some last-minute details as they prepared to part ways for the woods. Danny went first.

"Dad and I will take the buddy stand on the west end of the property. My phone is on if any of you need help dragging a deer out. Blessings on everyone. We'll see you around noon—or earlier if someone pulls a trigger."

After the other guys shared their general plans, the group finished up their pre-hunt ritual, split up, and disappeared into the pre-dawn darkness.

Danny quietly led his father away from the cabin and down a long, well-trimmed trail that followed a ridgeline. The distance they had to cover was about a quarter of a mile, and the terrain was relatively level. As the small, bluish flashlight beam bounced along the ground in front of Danny's feet, his heart was filled with joy at the sound of his dad following right behind him. He stopped briefly and turned to speak. Before he could say a word, his dad had something to say.

"It's darker than the inside of a coffin out here, Danny. I'm glad you brought a light for me to use."

"We're almost there, Dad, and with plenty of time to spare before legal shooting light. This ridge stand has yielded some really good deer in the past five years we've hunted from this place. I hope we see a buck, but for herd health some does need to be culled, so whatever comes by first is yours to take."

Jerry flinched a little at the thought of actually killing a doe...or any deer for that matter. It wasn't something he had a hankering to do, but being here in this setting that his son was passionate about was very important to him. He nodded his agreement and said, "Okay. Got it."

Within 10 minutes the two men ascended the ladder of the two-man deer stand and sat down to wait for shooting light.

Danny whispered softly, "If we see something this morning, it will likely come from our right. At night the deer like to feed in a field about 100 yards away. They usually come through these woods to get to a thicket on our left. That's their daytime bedding area. So check to your right often, and I'll watch the left side."

"What do I do if I see something, son?"

Danny realized he'd forgotten to cover the steps to take if a deer was spotted approaching the stand area. He thought quickly how to make the tutoring brief. "Basically, don't make any quick moves. Deer have keen eyesight and are very alert and nervous. When you lift your gun to fire, move slowly like a snail. And you might get a little excited when the moment of truth comes. I still do, and I've been doing this for a while. That can make holding the gun steady a bit of a challenge."

"What do you mean by 'moment of truth'?" his dad asked.

"That's what hunters call it when the time comes to take the shot. It can mess with your nerves. Some people turn real shaky when it happens. They look a little like Barney Fife at a bank robbery. But you'll do fine."

Jerry smiled tentatively at the explanation, and then he looked to his right into the semi-darkness of the woods. He wondered what he would do when he faced the "moment of truth."

Finally the morning sky turned pale blue. A few minutes later Danny whispered, "Shooting light is here, Dad. Anytime from now till sunset is legal hunting hours. Keep your eyes open. We'll need to be very quiet now."

Jerry could hear tension in his son's whisper, but as he replayed the sound in his mind, he realized that Danny wasn't feeling tension; instead, it was joyous anticipation. Jerry knew very well the huge difference between the two emotions. One had the potential to cause ulcers, and the other could bring a satisfying sense of expectation to a soul, the kind that can heal an ulcer. Suddenly it occurred to him that there might be a whole lot more to deer hunting than just shooting deer. Feeling the same wave of excitement his boy was enjoying, Jerry turned his eyes to the right and watched the woods carefully.

There was only an occasional word whispered between the two of them as they watched for deer. Jerry had feared that the sitting and waiting that is part of the hunting experience would bore him to tears, but when he looked at his watch and saw that an hour had passed seemingly quicker than a minute, he admitted his thoughts to his son. "I can't believe we've been sitting here an hour already," he whispered. "It went by in a flash. I guess it's all the stuff that is here to entertain a fellow. That sunrise was unbelievable as it came through the trees. And I bet I've seen at least a half-dozen bird species. Plus, I had no idea that chipmunks could be so busy— and noisy too. This is great!"

Danny smiled as his dad talked so favorably about what he'd seen that morning. "It really is amazing what all goes on in the living room of nature. It's almost as busy as a city out here. One of my favorite parts of the hunt is sitting and watching the show. I…"

Danny's eyes suddenly got big. He stopped talking as he looked over his dad's shoulder in the direction of the field. "Dad, there are three deer coming toward us—two bucks and a doe. Slowly turn your head, and I guarantee you'll see 'em."

Jerry's muscles tensed as he slowly moved his face toward the deer. He felt his head jerking a little with the adrenaline that suddenly surged through him. Before he saw the trio of deer, he heard the faint sounds of their steps in the dry leaves. It sounded like a group of people walking through the woods. He knew he couldn't detect the distinctness of the noise the way Danny probably could, but the audio was thrilling to hear.

The deer stopped briefly to browse for some residual acorns under a huge, red oak. Danny took the opportunity to coach his dad through the next step of the hunt.

"Dad, as slowly as you can, move the rifle up and look through the scope. At the same time, slowly shift around to your right. Try really hard to not make any noise." Danny's heart was pounding like a symphony kettledrum, and he wondered if his dad was feeling the same rush of emotion.

"Son, I'm shaking like a leaf." Jerry's voice was barely audible.

"That's okay, Dad. It's normal and part of the hunt! Rest your elbows on the railing and take a deep breath. One of the bucks is a nice eight point. He's plenty bigger than the other buck. He's the one you want to get. Let me know when you have him in your scope."

Jerry had to fight the unfamiliar battle with nerves—"buck fever," he decided. He struggled to hold the gun steady on the buck.

Danny listened to his dad's heavy breathing and knew he was experiencing more than just a little piece of the adrenaline pie that comes with deer hunting. In fact, Danny figured his dad was chowing down the whole pie.

"I've got him in my scope! Where do I aim?"

"I'm looking at him through my binoculars too. He's broadside just like you need him to be. Now, move the crosshairs to a spot just barely behind his front shoulder and about eight inches above the underline of his belly. That's your target. Now, push the safety button forward. When you feel your aim is steady, slowly squeeze the trigger. Don't anticipate the kick; instead, let the gun surprise you when it goes off."

Five seconds later the ladder stand rattled as a shot rang out and Jerry experienced the kick of the .30-06.

"Jack another shell into the chamber, Dad, and get the scope back to your eye!" Danny encouraged. "You might need to take another shot."

Jerry wrestled with the gun to reload. He peered through the scope again. "I don't see anything. The deer are gone."

Danny kept looking at the area through his binoculars. "Two of them are gone, Dad, but one of them is lying on the other side of that red oak! He's hard to spot, but I can see some white hair on the ground." He lowered his glasses, stood up in the stand, and looked down at his father. "Dad, you're the man today! You just got yourself a really nice eight-point buck."

"You're kidding!" Jerry looked toward where the buck was supposedly lying. He looked back at his son. "Are you serious?"

"Serious as a heart attack, Dad! He's brown and down. You need a high-five and a big hug, but we'd better get on the ground to celebrate. I'm so pumped I'm about to fall out of this treestand!"

On the ground, the father and son embraced and then headed toward the red oak. After several minutes of admiring the heavy-beamed, eight-point rack on the buck and retelling the details of how the kill came about,

Danny forced out the question he was afraid to ask. "What do you think of this deer huntin' thing, Dad? Is it anything like you imagined?"

Jerry thought for a few seconds. "Son, I have only two things to say in answer to your question. One, when I heard you say those deer were coming in and I turned to take the shot, I thought my heart was going to leap out of my jacket. I haven't been that nervous since I asked your mama to marry me. The second thing I have to say is 'when does deer season start next year?' You gotta let me come back and do this again!"

Danny's face felt like it would break in half as he grinned at his dad. "You have no idea how welcome you are to join us on this mountain, Dad. I'm so excited and pleased that we...that *you*...have discovered you are a born hunter. The way you handled the challenge of keeping calm enough to take a solid shot was amazing. Only a true deer hunter could pull that off. There's a ton to learn about this huntin' thing, and I would be beyond thrilled to show you everything I know about it."

Jerry smiled. "And I'd be more than thrilled to let you show me. This is a new day for me...for us. One I'm really glad I've lived to see."

Danny took out his cell phone to call his mom and tell her what had just happened. As he touched the numbers on the keypad, he remembered the hesitation he'd felt two weeks earlier about phoning his dad. A shiver went up his spine at the thought that he almost hadn't dialed the numbers and extended the invitation. As the phone rang, he looked across the body of the big buck at his dad, who was still admiring his trophy. Danny silently prayed, "Thank You, God, for helping me make the call. Thank You!"

That's a Call

Hey, Pop, how you been?
I'm coming to see you again.
I'm leaving in the morning, gonna drive straight through.
By the time the sun goes down, I'll be pulling into town.
We'll go to dinner at the diner, just me and you.

That's a call he's so glad he made,
'Cause heaven knows how much regrets can weigh.
Things unsaid, things undone,
They pile up till they weigh a ton
On the heart every day.
That's a call he's so glad he made.

Hey, boss, change of plans.
Tonight I'll be driving back in.
A day early, but don't worry—I'm gonna close that deal.
But there's a place I gotta be, sitting right there in the seats
At the kickoff, yelling my head off.
It's my boy's first game.

That's a call he's so glad he made
'Cause heaven knows how much regrets can weigh.
Things unsaid, things undone,
They pile up till they weigh a ton
On the heart every day.
That's a call he's so glad he made.

Hello, I know it's getting late,
But before you drive back tomorrow
I just need to tell you that I love you.
Be careful on the road.
I can't wait to hug you when you get back home.

That's a call he's so glad he made
'Cause heaven knows how much regrets can weigh.
Things unsaid, things undone,
They pile up till they weigh a ton
On the heart every day.
That's a call he's so glad he made.[1]

5

The Connection

by Paul Meeks

There he was, standing in the middle of the small food plot, grinning ear-to-ear and giving me an exuberant thumbs-up. The scene is burned into my memory banks forever. The year was 1991. It was October, and the elated 11-year-old deer hunter was my son Ilar Paul Meeks. He'd just made what he proudly described as a "perfect" shot on a big doe. It was his first bow kill.

Looking back, I remember what a radical change it was when my son started hunting with me. When he was only nine, he asked for a bow. And without consulting me, he announced he was going to start bowhunting with his ol' dad. I'd studied his face as he made the declaration, and it didn't take me but a few seconds to figure out that my days of enjoying the magical experience of entering the hunting woods alone with nothing on my mind but outsmarting a big buck had come to an end. From then on I knew my mission would be to outfit a nine-year-old with a bow, teach him to shoot, get him awake, coax him to get dressed at the ungodly hour of four in the morning, and head out to the hunter's woods. I was well aware there would be other challenges too, such as having to set up a separate treestand for him that would be within seeing distance (more like touching distance!) from my own. Yep, no more peaceful, unaccompanied hunts for me. Honestly though, I didn't mind at all.

To my surprise, after the first hunt with my new "bowhunting buddy," I quickly and willingly set my own big buck quest aside and became totally consumed with helping him get his first shot at a deer. Finally, the opportunity came, but an unexpected and unwelcomed problem arose. At nine years old he took a shot at a big doe. We watched the arrow hit perfectly in the lung area, but then watched as it fell to the ground. The arrow had barely broken the doe's skin. My little buddy could only pull 30 pounds with his compound bow, a pull weight that matched his muscles but didn't create enough kinetic energy with the light-aluminum arrows to make a kill. A river of boyhood tears ran down his cheeks that morning, and I had to fight hard to keep my composure. I don't know who was the most disappointed.

In his tenth year, my "bowhunter in the making" had gained quite a bit of strength and had moved up to a 40-pound bow. This time when deer appeared he found himself dealing with a terribly annoying case of the beginner bowhunter "yips," otherwise known as buck fever. As a result, he punctured a lot of ground instead of deer. He also managed to lose a noticeable number of arrows, and they aren't cheap.

When my hunting partner called to tell me he'd once again shot planet Earth instead of a whitetail that was only 15 yards away, I would sometimes respond with Philippians 4:6: "Be anxious for nothing, but in everything by prayer and supplication with thanksgiving let your requests be made known to God." He graciously accepted my repeated encouragement and promised that he'd try harder next time.

When his eleventh birthday came, Ilar Paul had not only moved up to a 45-pound bow, but he'd developed a lot of discipline and confidence in his shooting and hunting skills. It was amazing to watch him stand perfectly still, with or without a deer beneath his stand, fully confident that he could make the shot if an opportunity came. And finally it did. Neither of us will forget the day he made a clean pass-through shot at a sizeable Louisiana doe. While there wasn't a rack to tout, the deer was a huge trophy for my son—and for his dad too! From then on our course was set. We knew we had countless trips to the woods ahead of us to enjoy.

As always happens when raising children, time and experiences changed our lives. The cutting of the strings with the sharp scissors of school and all the activities that go with it occurred. Ilar Paul became quite an athlete. His involvement in high school sports included football, basketball, baseball, and the most mind-consuming sport of all—chasing girls (I thank the Lord that my son didn't catch one until much later when he was more mature). After graduation, he went straight into college and spent the next five years taking classes and participating in the Mississippi College football program. Life took an even more attention-getting turn for him when he met beautiful Brooke, the love of his life. He'd found a genuine Southern belle from a fine Christian family.

I was thrilled with my son's excellent choice for a bride, but their courtship and ensuing marriage basically ensured the extension of the change in the tight connection I'd had with my son.

I'd like to report that Ilar Paul settled into marriage and we were able to get back to doing some serious hunting together, but our road to making more memories in the deer stand took yet another detour. We immersed ourselves in trying to get our new outdoor accessories business, Great Day, Inc., up and running. And since we started it during a struggling economy, the task required countless hours of hard work and all the creativity and faith we could muster to keep the momentum going. We were business partners but our "hunting buddy" status suffered a great deal.

After a very long season of putting our efforts into launching the products we created and marketed, we both agreed that we were way overdue for a break. It was time to pick up where we'd left off a few years before. And we were determined to make up for lost time. That's when I brought up the idea of returning to the state of Kansas, where we'd hunted years before. It's an area known for its healthy-sized bucks. Thankfully, Ilar Paul agreed that we should set our sights on that goal.

The two of us managed to get our calendars synchronized so we could be in the Sunflower state for the first week of rut season. It would be just us—no cameramen and no other hunters in camp. Just the two of us spending concentrated time chasing big bruisers and catching up on each other's lives. After a thorough job of packing our needed gear, we were off to what we considered a small piece of hunter heaven.

The 11-hour ride from Tallulah, LA, to Kiowa, KS, gave us a pretty good chunk of catch-up time. To my delight, a good portion of Ilar Paul's contribution to our conversation was spent fondly recalling many of our past hunts, as well as expressing the ways he was thankful for the good things in his life he was enjoying. It blessed my heart to hear him speak with such a humble tone about God's provision and guidance. His words warmed me like a campfire on a chilly night. I could have basked in them for the rest of the trip. But then we saw a mile marker that told us we weren't far from the farm we'd be hunting on. Our conversation suddenly took a turn from the joys and challenges of life to the big bucks that were known to roam this area.

As we rode along, we started laying out a strategy for the hunting days ahead. And, as though not one day had passed since he was 11, I returned to being the daddy I was to him back then. I said, "I want to put you in the best stand—the prime location where the odds will be highest for you to take a genuine trophy buck."

Ilar Paul was very understanding of my parenting attempt. He said that even though he appreciated my wish to put him in the top spot, he had his own ideas about where to hunt. After considering all the existing treestand setups on the property, plus the option of installing new treestands or ground blinds in new locations, he announced that he wanted to hunt the "big tree" stand.

The "big tree" stand was aptly named for the size of the old, river-bottom elm that held it. In its gigantic branches was an API Magnum Baby Grand that towered about 18 feet off the ground. It was an extremely dependable setup that I'd used successfully several times for filming hunts for television shows. I smiled at my son's show of independence and agreed with his decision. We both knew if he were patient, his time in the big elm was sure to pay off.

The first morning I dropped my son off at the "big tree" stand. Like a doting dad does, I watched him make his way up the gnarly old tree and strap himself securely in the safety harness. Feeling sure he was safe and settled in, I headed out to my stand of choice. Nothing happened in those initial hours, so we connected via radios and agreed on a lunch break at eleven o'clock. By two in the afternoon, we were back in the same stands.

This was a routine we followed for two days plus the first half of the third day. With neither of us seeing anything we considered "shooters," my patience was running a little on the thin side. Ilar Paul stuck to his guns, however, and headed back to the "big tree" for the afternoon hunt. Trying to follow my own advice and exercise some patience, I headed back to my stand. Again the afternoon was uneventful—only a couple of "wannabe" trophies passed my way.

As the sun began to set and shooting light faded, I climbed down from my stand, made my way back to the truck, and headed for the monster elm to pick up my boy. We only had one more hunting day left. When I pulled up, I could see Ilar Paul was already on the ground and had his gear piled up neatly at the base of the tree. Assuming he was ready to head back to camp, I waited in the truck, expecting him to gather up his stuff and get in. Then I saw it! That big, familiar grin I'd seen when he was 11 and had just arrowed his first deer. I turned the motor off, jumped out of the truck, and rushed over to where he stood. "Well, where is he?" I asked.

"He's right over here, Dad! I made a really good shot. But don't get too excited 'cause he's just an average-sized deer." I didn't notice the sly grin he was speaking through. I fell for his trick and responded with the line that every bowhunter uses to console a partner who connects with a critter he feels might not qualify for his wall of fame. "Well, Son, any bow kill is a trophy."

We walked about 30 yards, and when he shined his light on his deer I knew I'd been had. And I couldn't have been more happy about it! We gave each other a rowdy high-five and then stood there admiring the heavy 10-pointer we guessed would gross around 165 Pope & Young points. (We eventually had it scored, and the outcome was 168!)

After a couple of bear hugs, we got the deer loaded and headed to camp. During the ride, I got to hear every moment-by-moment detail of the hunt, including the mental calisthenics that Ilar Paul had used to overcome the yips. My excited son was so thrilled about his trophy that he thanked me at least a half-dozen times on the short drive for planning the hunt in such a productive place.

The next morning a storm front moved in and threatened a downpour. Even though I'd forgotten to bring rain gear, I headed for my stand. I was putting pressure on myself because of my son's success. It was time for me to make something happen. By midmorning the deer started moving ahead of the front, as they often do. I had two bucks pass by that were tempting to shoot but just not what I was looking for. I was watching an ominous dark cloud looming off to the west when out of nowhere a huge 10-pointer wandered in and passed right under my stand. It only took a few seconds to decide to take him and, with only a 20-yard shot, my arrow found its mark. The hefty buck went down within a few yards from where

I'd arrowed him. My hands shook with the post-shot yips as I dug for my radio to call Ilar Paul. I couldn't wait to tell him what had happened. When he answered, I could hear in his voice the thrill he felt for me as he offered his congratulations.

With our trophies cleaned and iced down, we celebrated with a great meal and a good night of sleep. After making short work of packing and reloading the truck early the next morning, we headed home to Louisiana.

Needless to say, the trip was a pleasant one—each of us describing and reliving every detail of the hunt we'd just completed. As we rode along laughing, talking, and soaking in our experiences, I realized once more how incredibly precious the time is that we get to spend with our children.

Sometime after that unforgettable trip to Kansas, I made a determination that was inspired by reading Genesis 3:9: "Then the LORD God called to [Adam], and said to him, 'Where are you?'" It seems that God, the heavenly Father, recognized that the gap had widened between His created son, Adam, and Him. Instead of waiting for Adam to initiate a restoration of their fellowship, God made the first move. In the case of Adam, the division was due to sin. When it came to my connection with Ilar Paul, the distance that had come between us was due simply to the busyness of life, yet it still felt just as dividing. When I pondered our situation, I realized it would be wise for me to be the one who made the effort to reattach the wires of communication between us. To do so was to follow the example of how our heavenly Father desires to keep the connection strong with His children. Striving to be a father like Him is always wise.

6

We'll Meet at "The Lodge"

by Chad Gilliland

My only sibling, Lee, and I were raised in central Montana. Though he was the older of the two of us, we were equals when it came to how much we enjoyed being outside on the wind-swept plains of our Big Sky state. The extreme seasonal weather conditions of our region often made certain activities a formidable challenge for two youngsters, but we didn't hesitate to brave the elements, especially when another big-game hunting season rolled around. We looked forward to it with optimism and great expectations.

Our father, Hubert, loved taking *his* boys and teaching them how to hunt. He always favored the beautiful, wind-protected mountains located two hours from our home. The geography was, and still is, pure Montana. Like many others, we refer to it as "God's country," a perfect mixture of rugged, majestic mountains and lush lowlands. The territory was easily accessible via logging roads that wound through a blend of aspen groves and tall pines. There were also many grassy meadows within the mountain drainages that attracted the bigger game. This section of Montana held boundless opportunities for finding whitetail, mule deer, and elk. Taking game such as this was a high priority for us, and we provided plenty of meat for the family.

I never totally fell in love with the early morning wakeup calls and the two-hour drives in the dark that were required to get to our favorite hunting spot before daylight. I would have gladly done without the necessity of enduring the finger-numbing low temperatures in the hopes of filling our tags. Lee and my father, however, never seemed to be bothered by such demanding conditions. They simply loved everything about our adventures. And it was their unbridled excitement that spilled over into my heart and kept me tagging along with them.

I was way too young to recognize it back then, but when I look back on those days I can see that what my dad and brother enjoyed most about our trips was more than just the hiking and hunting. They found that the closeness between the three of us was best cultivated while we were in the wild. That was, by far, the greatest trophy for them and for me. I wish I'd realized and relished this much more through the years.

For reasons none of us will understand until we "get home to heaven," God called my brother away at the young age of 38. When the news of Lee's unexpected passing reached our ears, the ultimate solace our family found was trusting that our Savior's plan is always good. We said our tear-drenched farewells to Lee, and in time we moved forward with life. One thing we determined to do, though, was continue Lee's godly legacy here on earth. One of the best ways to accomplish that goal was to keep the stories of our hunts with him alive by sharing them with those who loved him and passing them down to the next generation.

One story I like to recall and retell involved a deer hunt Lee, Dad, and I went on that was near the town of Lincoln, Montana. It yielded an encounter with some rather intense emotions as well as a particularly unforgettable life lesson. Lee was a teenager, and I was 12 at the time.

After an unsuccessful morning hunt on a parcel of public land, the three of us gathered at "The Hunting Lodge," the name we'd given to our dad's well-used, 1980-era 4 x 4 Ford F-150 pickup truck. We were there for a sack lunch and a short nap.

Being the one in the threesome who had a tendency to pack it in if nothing was happening, I voted to start home and "road hunt" along the way. The thought of heading back out for a long, afternoon hike just for a relatively short evening hunt didn't sound all that exciting to me, especially since it would require a long walk back in the dark. Unfortunately, my idea was quickly overruled. Lee never lost hope that a trophy animal might come out of his wooded bedding area before sunset and step into a meadow for a pre-moonlight graze. I could always tell that Dad was proud of Lee's determination and optimism. Somehow he seemed to know that those virtues would eventually rub off on me. And he was right.

As we prepared for the evening hunt, Dad surprised us when he suggested that Lee and I go out together without him. He would venture off on his own and meet us back at "The Lodge" after sunset. He assured us that the full moon that night would help us navigate our way back to our gathering spot.

Now that I'm a father, I look back and realize that our dad's decision to let his 14-year-old and 12-year-old hunt without him could not have been an easy one. But by allowing us to explore and hike around the area with him well before we could carry a rifle, he'd been preparing us for this day when he let out the leash. He was confident that we were familiar enough with the terrain to not get lost. Though he believed we were ready to strike out on our own, it was still a lot of responsibility to put on two boys who were so young.

I didn't see it at the time, but the level of confidence Dad had in Lee's leadership was high. He admitted to me later that he'd had second thoughts about challenging those skills, but he pushed them aside and prayed for us as we made our plans for the evening hunt. I recall that my brother and I felt a collective peace about the idea of being together alone in the woods. I distinctly remember us both feeling emboldened by Dad's actions and trust. What I didn't know was just how much Lee felt the weight of the responsibility Dad had placed on him to get *both* of us back to the truck. And neither of us could have anticipated what would happen to test our steel that evening.

The strategy was for Lee and me to hike back to a place we called the "first meadow," about a half-mile from the truck. We'd find a good location to sit patiently and see if anything would come our way. For Lee, the waiting game was easy since he seemed blessed with a calm demeanor. Patience was normally within easy grasp whenever he needed it. The same couldn't be said about me. The idea of sitting still for the entire evening wasn't something I considered a load of fun. Still, I conceded to the plan.

Lee told Dad that he thought the best stand for us would be the remains of an old log cabin located in the far back corner of the meadow.

The structure was just a shell of what it once was, and only two or three feet of the perimeter walls were still standing. He believed it would provide good cover as well as open sight lines for shots.

Dad agreed with Lee about hunting at the old cabin site. With everyone's intended whereabouts stated, we all left The Lodge together. After climbing over a fence and walking along the abandoned logging road a short distance, we came to a "Y." We stopped and once again reviewed the plans for the evening. Dad reminded us to not go anywhere we hadn't discussed. He also reminded us that if we were going to be late back to the truck to fire a shot so he'd know we were coming.

Dad took off to the left, and Lee and I headed to the right. I still remember watching Dad walk away until I could no longer see spots of his hunter orange vest through the trees. I was thankful I had Lee to rely on. He seemed happy to have my company, a mutual feeling that never changed as we grew up.

It took us about 30 minutes to arrive at the cabin and get situated for the next couple of hours of hunting. The front side of the cabin faced an open meadow. Lee sat in the front right corner; I positioned myself in the front left corner about 10 feet from him. We were both comfortable but ready for action. I don't remember what we quietly talked about that evening as we watched the meadow and tree lines for movement, but I remember doing most of it. Lee graciously endured my whispered ramblings as he silently scanned the area.

We each had our own backpacks, and since we weren't seeing anything I started digging through mine to see how many snack-sized Snickers bars might be tucked away in the bottom. Lee never lost his focus on the challenge of bagging a deer.

Time passed slowly for me, but I'm sure far too quickly for Lee. In my opinion it was getting late enough to start gathering my things for the hike out. I looked forward to getting back to The Lodge, where we would once again meet up with Dad. I suddenly heard some subdued-yet-intentional sounds of movement. I looked over to my right to find Lee, but he was no longer there. I quickly turned more to the right and saw that he'd moved to the back corner of the cabin and had found a solid rest for his rifle. He was alert and ready to fire. I wondered, *What does he see? Why didn't he tell me what was happening?*

I discovered that he'd been watching a few whitetail does playing along the tree line behind us for several minutes. He thought he'd spotted a young buck, but it took some time to be sure the deer had antlers. The daylight was beginning to fade as he patiently waited for the deer to turn broadside. In the same instant that I decided to shift around to watch what he was doing, he squeezed the trigger. My entire body jumped at the unexpected sound of the explosion. A few seconds later Lee lifted his eye from the scope and did what he had done before when I was present after he fired at a deer. He turned and looked at me, nodded his head up and down, and gave me a confident smile. I knew he'd connected. I silently returned a big smile of congratulations.

Lee and I quickly checked our gun safeties just like Dad had taught us to do. We grabbed our gear. It wasn't a long walk to the heavily wooded area where the wounded buck had escaped after the shot. There was a fair amount of deadfall on the forest floor, but thankfully we found the deer quickly. We both wanted to bask in the glow of the kill, but we had no time to feel proud. Darkness was coming fast.

We didn't say much to each other as we began working on the task at hand that had to be completed before the fullness of night came. Neither of us would admit it, but one of the reasons we hurried was that it was a bit unnerving to be in the woods after dark without Dad at our side. We fought the eerie feelings and continued the field-dressing process. I remember being a bit jealous of how efficiently Lee handled the sharp knife and how skillfully he tied ropes on the buck's legs for the drag back to the truck. I looked forward to learning all that he already knew.

The decision we made next became a memory we enjoyed later in life and laughed about through the years. Instead of dragging the deer on a level, unobstructed-but-longer route back to The Lodge, we decided to drag it up and over the deadfall inside the timber. This would allow us a straight line to the truck. We were sure it would be quicker even though we knew it would take a lot more effort.

When we began pulling the deadweight of the deer, our hands were full so we weren't able to use our flashlights, which made the progression toward The Lodge even harder and more daunting. Not too far into the dragging, we quickly became winded and tired. We stopped for a breather, but when we heard the coyotes howl not too far away we found a new surge of energy. I nervously laughed with Lee when he mentioned the fact that we were dragging coyote bait! We didn't confess until later, but both of us had chill bumps on our chill bumps as we huffed our way through the predator-infested timber.

In response to the fear we were feeling, each time we stopped to improve our hold on the ropes, we would quickly "re-grip and go." Finally we decided to not even stop for rest breaks. We didn't even stop long enough for sips of water or to remove some layers of clothing to help cool off.

Dad had heard the lone shot from Lee's rifle. He figured one of us had gotten a deer, but he chose to stick to his plan and return to the truck instead of trying to find us. He told us later that he anxiously counted the minutes that seemed to pass like hours as he waited for the two of us to return.

At one point during the back-breaking dragging of the buck, Lee became frustrated with my inability to keep up so he very decisively handed me our guns and packs, grabbed his deer by the rack with both hands, and started dragging it by himself. He was a well-built, strong young man for his age. After what seemed like an eternity, we finally broke out of the timber and found the logging road.

Dragging the carcass on the open roadbed was so much easier! Lee was pleased when I chipped in again with the pulling, and we quickly recognized when we'd made it back to the "Y" in the road. It was just a short distance from the gated fence where the truck was parked. As we approached The Lodge, we saw the darkened outline of a bright, hunter-orange sweatshirt. It was Dad! Our spirits lifted instantly. When he saw us, he smiled wide and threw his arms out to welcome us back. His outpouring of praise and pride met our ears.

Dad listened to my version of the hunt as he admired the nice buck we'd dragged in. He commended me for braving the dark and for being such a help to Lee with the hard work it took to get the beast field dressed and back to The Lodge. Then he turned to Lee and commended him for his display of solid skills in deciding where to set up, waiting patiently for the deer to present itself for an effective broadside shot, and leading us back successfully.

The two of us were pleased that Dad had trusted us to go out on our own for the first time. We thanked him for his willingness to sacrifice his own comfort to let us do something so grown-up.

Needless to say, Lee and I were totally worn out when we climbed into the cab of The Lodge for the trip back to our house. Typically, Lee and I would have been asleep before we reached the paved road, but that wasn't the case on this drive. Every mile was packed with the telling and retelling of the details of the evening hunt. Dad laughed out loud again about the chills we got when we heard the howls of the coyotes and how Lee had pointed out we were pulling coyote bait through the darkness.

As the years went by following that unforgettable hunt, the three of us talked about it from time to time. Whenever the adventure came up in our conversation, Lee and I would thank Dad again for using that day as a teaching moment to instill a new level of confidence in us. We also reminded him about the poignant welcome he gave us that night, a reflection of the moment when our heavenly Father will welcome His children home. Little did Dad and I know that such a moment would come much sooner for Lee than we thought. Today he is indeed a missed son and brother, but because of Christ we know we'll meet him again someday at The Lodge in heaven.

7

My Rack Hunter

by Steve Chapman

My daughter, Heidi, stopped me in my tracks, put her hand on my forearm, and softly said, "Dad, there it is! Straight ahead...do you see it?" Her voice had an excited tremor. I could hardly believe how quickly she was able to spot the trophy we'd been looking for during our hunt. The area where we were had an endless pattern of colors to test even the keenest of vision, but her eyes were well trained by experience.

She looked around to make sure there were no other hunters in the area and whispered, "That's the same one I saw two days ago. I'm sure of it. I just hope no one else has a bead on it. We gotta move!"

Confident that our long hunt was about to meet with success, I fell in behind my daughter as she began a determined stalk. I knew she was about to explode with excitement and that it wasn't easy for her to resist breaking into a run. After weaving our way through a thick stand of obstacles, we managed to get within shooting distance. That's when I heard the gun go off.

Cha-ching!

It was followed by, "That'll be $89.99 plus tax, please."

The smoke drifted from the barrel of my credit card as Heidi smiled and admired the dress that we'd just bagged.

"Now this is the way to hunt, Dad. I find 'em and you shoot 'em for me. And don't you like that it's already cleaned and hangin' up?"

"Yes, Heidi. I wish deer hunting were as tidy as this, but after the two hours we've spent walking around this mall, I can tell you that your kind of hunting is a lot harder."

Heidi threw her trophy over her shoulder, and we headed to the car. We'd just finished another annual tradition that we'd enjoyed through the years—the annual birthday hunt for a dress. The cost of the trips to the mall with my expert "rack" hunter grew progressively more expensive as time went by, but the memories with Heidi are worth every dime I'll never see again.

Though Heidi is all girl and enjoys the pursuit of a trophy dress, she also loves the outdoors, especially fishing. In years past we've wet our lines in waters from the Gulf of Mexico to the Atlantic, from off the coast of Miami to the Pacific Ocean, from off Canada's outer banks to the lakes in Tennessee. While angling is her preference, thankfully she appreciates my passion for hunting wild game. One year she went with me on a springtime turkey hunt. It was a hunt that yielded a memory I still enjoy recalling.

We got to the farm where we were going to hunt about two hours after daylight. Normally I like to be in the area where the gobblers are before the sun rises, but knowing that a four o'clock wakeup call would not contribute to Heidi's affection for the hunt, I'd deliberately delayed our arrival to the woods. Furthermore, I knew by the time we got there the hens would be nearing their midmorning preoccupation with their nests, which would, in turn, make it easier to entice the lovesick toms with my turkey calling. In addition, Heidi wouldn't have to spend a lot of time sitting in one spot since the strategy was to walk around and do some contact calling.

After 45 minutes or so of checking out a few of the lower fields on the property and then ascending a hill via a logging road, a gobbler finally responded to the sound of my slate call.

"Quick!" I said as I slipped off the logging road and into the woods. "Follow me. We gotta find a spot just off this road, sit down, and get ready. I think that bird might come in."

Heidi could tell I was jazzed by the sound of the gobbler. She seemed to share in my excitement.

"What do I do, Dad?" she asked when we found our spot.

"Just sit next to me and get comfortable. And whatever you do, if I say

'Don't move,' then don't move. The eyesight of a turkey is amazing. They can see everything…they see almost as good as you when you spot a dress from a mile away."

She understood the comparison and smiled as she pulled the mesh camo mask I'd loaned her down over her face. Within a few minutes the gobbler responded again to my call. I guessed it was probably around 60 yards away. The lush, late-April foliage was so thick I couldn't get a visual.

"He's pretty close, Heidi, so don't move."

She cooperated and kept looking in the direction my face was pointed.

As gobblers often do, the bird hung up just out of sight and wouldn't come in. I knew he was out there staging, strutting, and waiting for the hen he'd heard to come to him. Seconds turned to minutes, and before I knew it 10 minutes had gone by. The turkey gobbled occasionally at my quiet yelps, but it was obvious he hadn't advanced any further toward us.

"We gotta wait this bird out, Heidi. If you don't mind, let's stay right here for a while."

"I'm fine with it, Dad. This is kinda fun!"

Another few minutes and a few stubborn gobbles went by as we sat quietly against the huge oak. I was enjoying this rare opportunity to be on a hunt with Heidi. I smiled at the thought and then found my thoughts drifting from the nearby bird to a time when Heidi was still a baby. I recalled a detail that I decided might explain why she was so good at dress hunting.

When Annie and I had our two children back in the late 1900s, ultrasound technology was reserved primarily for examinations of pre-born babies with medical concerns. For that reason, we didn't know in advance what the sex of our newborns would be. That was fine with me. Though we couldn't plan our nursery colors and choose a specific name in advance of the births, I enjoyed the mystery of boy or girl that grew with each passing month of Annie's pregnancies.

Our firstborn, Nathan, was nearing three years old when we learned we were expecting a second child. He began campaigning for a brother. Annie conceded that another boy would be a good sibling for our son, and she joined Nathan in his prayers for a boy baby. Not me! I longed to have a little girl in our home. I was so hopeful that the newborn would be a daughter that I went to a department store, marched straight to the children's clothing section, and planned to get a dress for my new baby girl. It was my act of faith that God would hear my prayer request.

I wandered up and down the aisles until I finally saw a dress that gave me that "ah-ha!" feeling. It had a velvety black top, a red-plaid skirt, and a matching plaid bow sewn on at the waistline. Without even looking at the price tag, I bought it. I was quite proud of my find, but what I didn't know was that I'd purchased a dress that would fit an 18-month-old child. All I knew was that it looked small and really pretty.

When I got home, Annie nearly went into labor from laughing at my uneducated attempt at shopping for a young female.

"This is so sweet," she said, "but do you know how dangerous it is to buy a dress for a female that is three times the size she needs?"

I gave her a puzzled look.

"A purchase like that can send a gal the kind of message that can get a fellow in some deep doo-doo. Just be glad you didn't get me a dress while you were out shopping today!"

I defended myself with my best shot. "It's not about the dress, babe. It's about who I'm hoping will wear it." Annie knew my wishes regarding the little one growing in her belly. She smiled and hugged me before dropping a bomb on me.

"I know how you are about never wanting to waste anything, so I gotta ask. What if our baby is another little boy? Are you gonna make him wear this dress?"

I didn't have a response other than, "Just make sure you have a girl." And with that, I took the dress and hung it in the nursery. And I prayed some more.

As it turned out, on April 15 my hope for adding a daughter to our family was filled. Annie went along with my choice for a name—Heidi Anne. As far as I was concerned, if the goal of mankind was to produce the perfect daughter, there was no need for anyone else on the planet to get pregnant. Heidi was it.

As experienced parents know, it didn't take long at all until Heidi grew into that dress. When we put it on her, Annie and I agreed that it was perfect for her. Heidi looked absolutely stunning in it.

Now, after the passage of many years, I was considering how my innate ability to find just the right dress had somehow been imprinted in her DNA. That means, of course, that I'm solely responsible for her tremendous rack hunting skills!

It seemed that in the flicker of a deer's tail, my little girl went from 18 months old to 16 years old! And now she was sitting beside me waiting for a turkey to strut closer. I looked over at her. *My how grown-up she seems and oh, how lovely. She's such a joy in my life…*

Suddenly another ground-rattling shout from the gobbler shook me back to the present and the hunt.

"Heidi," I whispered, moving nothing except my lips, "could you tell if that bird is closer? I think he's decided to come on in."

"I did notice he sounded louder. Don't move, right?"

"Absolutely. Not even a muscle, and if you can, don't even blink if he rounds the bend of this logging road 'cause he'll be within 25 yards of us."

I rested my shotgun on my knee. I could feel my heart pounding as I gently placed the tip of my index finger on the safety button. I was happily immersed in a pool of adrenaline. I couldn't wait until the red head of the gobbler appeared.

Just to be sure Heidi was doing okay, I slowly turned my head to check on her. What I saw was one of the main reasons she's such a delight to have in our family. She was adding a little comic relief to this otherwise tense moment. She'd lifted her left hand up to the bottom of her long, brown hair and was pushing up on it slowly but repeatedly. She was mocking the motion that a fancily dressed woman might do just before making a grand entrance into a ballroom. As she did, she looked at me through her mesh face mask.

I could see the mischievous glint in her eyes and the smile on her lips. I was pretty sure what was going on in her mind. "No way am I gonna miss this chance to mess with my daddy's head!" And mess with it, she did. When she saw my eyes widen at her antics, she snickered and whispered, "I gotta look good for the feller that's on his way."

Once again I'd been had by a master jokester. Actually, I should have expected it, but she always manages to surprise me with her well-timed antics, a skill she'd started developing at a young age. There are several more examples I could offer, but one of our family's favorites is when we had a dozen or so kids at our house for Nathan's eleventh birthday party. They had arrived at 11 o'clock, and each one brought a ravenous appetite for the pizza and chocolate cake Annie was planning to serve at lunchtime.

Heidi was about eight, and she was well aware that the combined level of hunger that our company felt was huge. Armed with that knowledge, she stepped out on the elevated deck at the back of our house around 11:30 and yelled down to the crowd of hungry youngsters, "Lunch is ready!"

Like a stampede of cattle, the kids ran for the basement door, nearly trampling each other as they entered the house. Once inside, the hungry little mob ran up the stairs and into the kitchen—only to find that not a morsel was ready for consumption. Heidi's eyes gleamed with satisfaction as she announced to the bunch, "Kidding!"

The kitchen filled with starved moans when the kids realized what had happened. As each child lowered his head in disappointment and headed back down the stairs, Heidi pulled her shoulders back and grinned maniacally from ear to ear. In fact, it was exactly the way she was grinning right now as we waited for the gobbler to appear.

I'd like to report that Heidi got to see that bird meet its Maker that day, but as it turned out the old tom decided to go in another direction. I'm confident he never knew we were there, but I'll always remember that time. In fact, I could take you to the very tree we were sitting against when the "Primp Queen" got me good. It remains one of my favorite moments in the woods.

Another time my daughter used her gift of making her old dad smile deserves a mention, but the occasion was far more emotionally intense than a battle of wits with a mature gobbler. Heidi needed a C-section to birth her second baby. Without knowing it, a small portion of the placenta was left in her uterus, resulting in some dangerously excessive post-birth bleeding. The medicine she was given seemed to have solved the problem, but about a week later, while at our house, she began to bleed profusely. Her husband, Emmitt, was out of town on a quick business trip, and I'd assumed the responsibility of rushing her to the hospital if necessary.

I called ahead and asked her doctor to meet us there. Heidi was growing weaker by the moment, and when we arrived at the hospital she was immediately given an IV of fluids and placed in a wheelchair to be taken to the surgery floor. The doctor didn't want to wait on a uniformed assistant, so she handed me the IV bag and instructed me to hold it high and run alongside Heidi.

We were hurrying down a hallway headed toward an elevator that would take us to the operating room when Heidi suddenly fainted. Dead to the world, her feet went straight out and dug into the carpeted floor, stopping her forward progress. Her doctor quickly reached inside her pocket, pulled out a packet of smelling salts, broke it open, and waved it under Heidi's nose. She roused briefly, and I was able to get her feet back up on the footboards of the wheelchair. We took off running again. When we reached the elevator, the doctor pushed the button several times, hoping to hurry its arrival. Finally the door opened, and we quickly went inside.

Heidi's head was back with her face toward the ceiling. I was glad to hear and see her stir a little. The doctor and I looked back and forth, moving our gaze from Heidi to the changing red numbers above the elevator door.

Heidi's enthusiastic voice broke the silence. "I see a bright light!"

My heart jumped into my throat. My assumption was that Heidi's life was fading away. Every muscle in my body tensed, and I was speechless. I looked at the doctor and noticed that her face had paled. She was staring at her patient with a look of sheer panic.

Then Heidi spoke again. I feared it might be her last words.

"Bright light, ya'll. Right there! See it? It's in the ceiling!" Then she pointed at the recessed florescent lighting above us and laughed. She lifted her head up and looked at her two victims, waiting for our reaction.

Her doctor offered a relieved chuckle and then gave a good-natured scolding to her patient for taking several years off her life. All I could do was sort of laugh. The level of joy I felt when I realized Heidi was feeling good enough to bring a little humor into the situation was monumental. She'd gotten us—and good.

We were still laughing, albeit a bit worriedly, when the elevator door opened. The nurse who met us there seemed a little puzzled as to why we were smiling, especially when she noticed the considerable amount of blood that was present. She took the IV bag from me and helped the doctor whisk my girl away to an operating room.

Needless to say, the time crawled by agonizingly slow. It seemed like hours as I waited for the doctor to reappear and give me the latest update. I stood quietly at a window and looked out at the city of Nashville. The tears rolled down my cheeks at the thought of losing Heidi. Thankfully, the outcome was positive. The portion of residual placenta was removed, and Heidi's condition improved quickly. I am so blessed to still have her around to "mess with my head" every once in a while!

As many parents have discovered, when it comes to getting a reminder of how precious our children are, there's hardly anything more effective than living through the trauma of nearly losing them or, worse yet, actually losing them. The gratitude I have that Heidi is still around is deep and rich. Though we don't get to do as much adventuring together as we used to enjoy, we still do the annual birthday "rack" hunt. The only difference now is that Heidi and Emmitt's three little "hunterettes" tag along. And believe me, they also are becoming incredible rack hunters. After all, it's in their DNA too! And it's becoming more and more apparent that the girls inherited Heidi's humor gene. We're in for quite a ride!

8

Through My Father's Eyes

by Paul Walerczak

As I sat in the woods with my son in the darkness of that early November morning, we both felt the anticipation growing like the light that was slowly illuminating the environment. For nearly a half hour we whispered our conversation and anxiously waited for shooting light. We talked mostly about how much we hoped this would be the day he would connect with his first whitetail.

Finally we were minutes away from first light. Our talking ceased. In the quiet, my thoughts raced over the previous two weeks of whitetail hunting. William, who was only eight years old at the time, had hunted hard with me, trying to take advantage of each and every valuable moment in his pursuit of harvesting his first deer. He was the hunter that morning; I was the cameraman and coach.

This epic game of cat and mouse with one of God's smartest animals, the whitetail deer, was taking place in southern Indiana's rolling hills. The valleys and agriculture fields provided a beautiful panorama of God's handiwork in this region of the world we called home. Will had been so close to taking a deer on numerous occasions over the two-week period of time, but each opportunity slipped through his hands for various unexpected reasons.

Several of the days we hunted were all-day vigils spent in a ground blind watching and waiting for that golden opportunity where skill, knowledge, God's intervention, and the hopes and dreams of a little boy would come together in a magical moment of time. While it might seem to some folks that what we were doing was a complete waste of time, what they don't realize is how my youngster was learning skills that would serve him well in the future. Through the long waits, for example, he was learning patience, persistence, and how to maintain a positive attitude. He was also seeing the value of hard work and, most important, gleaning a wealth of knowledge about his heavenly Creator.

As the morning sunlight fell on our camo-colored, pop-up blind, it warmed the interior. Questions ran through my mind. *Would my son receive the prize for all of his hard work and the huge effort required of such a young fellow during the past two weeks? Would he connect with his first whitetail? Would he be able to keep his composure enough to pull off a good shot? Would we even see a deer today?* As my thoughts raced, I uttered a simple prayer: "Lord, Your will be done today."

The reality of the situation that day was that it was highly possible for Will to harvest a trophy of a lifetime because of the location. This particular spot was simply one of God's perfect pieces of topography. Whitetails travel through this location often. In all my years of hunting, I don't know that I've found a setup as good as this one. The location is an inside corner on the top of a ridge with a beautiful, spring-fed stream running below the ridgeline before emptying into a larger river. Below the crest and across the stream there is a small crop field that is normally planted in beans or corn. The deer love to travel through this area as they move from a food source to a bedding area.

Good hunters know to look for signs that tell them a mature buck is in the area. Great hunters know how to find the signs and then read the topography of the land to anticipate how that buck will travel from point A to point B. The spot Will and I were in had a history of producing nice-sized, mature bucks. In fact, one had been harvested in that location just two weeks prior.

Everything seemed right for this to be the day Will would put his hands on a trophy whitetail. The spot, the wind, the frost, and the eagerness of my young son in whom I was well pleased seemed like the best ingredients for success. All we needed was an antlered passerby.

At 8:14, I turned the camera toward my son so he could provide an update on how the hunt was going. Like a professional who'd been filming his whole life, Will pulled down his mask, looked directly into the camera, and began to speak. A few seconds into his commentary he said, "We haven't seen any…" Just as he was forming the word "deer," I caught movement to my left. I quickly turned my head, swung the camera around, and said quietly, "Good buck! Good buck!"

Just like that there was a majestic whitetail moving along the ridge through the hardwoods and brush about 75 yards in front of us. He was followed by a small spike. The two had come up from the lower bottom by the stream and were now heading toward the bedding area.

My heart was pounding at a pace that rivaled the clatter of pistons in a fully revved diesel engine, and I'm sure Will's was too. When I looked over at my son and saw the rapid plumes of vapor coming from his mouth and filling the cool air around him, I knew his excitement level had skyrocketed. I also noticed that his hands and body were shaking. Yep, sure enough, he'd fallen victim to the "rack attack." It's a condition that warns an older hunter that a heart attack might be right around the corner. For a youngster like Will, the rack attack won't generate a coronary episode, but it may cause stammering lips, watery eyes, a confused daze, and trigger finger numbness. I guess the apple doesn't fall far from the tree, as they say. I'm staring 40 in the face, and I still get a little torn up when I see or hear a deer approaching my stand. In that moment I wondered if this would be the opportunity Will had been longing for. I tried to calm both of us down as I coached him on what was going to happen next.

The distance and type of cover the buck was moving through made a clean shot nearly impossible. We watched carefully as the animal walked at a steady pace, moving from our left to our right. Once he got into a position that hid us from him slightly, I picked up my grunt tube and issued a few guttural calls, followed by a very loud snort wheeze. The buck immediately stopped, snapped his head around, and looked intently in our direction. After what seemed like an eternity, he turned his head and continued on. The buck and the little spike slipped through the heavy cover, and we never saw them again.

Due to this fresh encounter, Will and I were charged with excitement and confidence even though that one had gotten away. We were positive our chosen spot was everything we'd hoped for. We still had three-and-a-half hours to hunt before we had to go home to fulfill familial obligations.

Surely we'd experience another encounter before the morning was over. You see, we had to because this was Will's last day to hunt this firearm season. It might even be the last whitetail hunt he could go on this year. Every now and then I silently sent a little prayer toward heaven: "Lord, Your will be done."

The minutes were passing by, and each tick of the second hand seemed like the pounding of a judge's gavel announcing the end of a court case. Several times Will asked, "Is it time to go yet, Dad?" I repeatedly responded, "There's plenty of time, Son. You need to remember it only takes a few seconds for the situation to change. There's plenty of time for you to harvest your first whitetail!"

One last time Will asked, "Is it time to go, Dad?"

I knew the time had come to say what he didn't want to hear and I didn't want to admit. I took a deep breath and swallowed hard. "Yes, Will. We need to pack up and head on home."

No river was deep and long enough to contain the emotions that followed. Will looked down for a few seconds, raised his head, and then turned toward me. Big tears were streaming down his small cheeks. As his father, I knew exactly what he was feeling. I was feeling it too, and my tears showed him that it was okay and fitting to be emotional. In that moment the phrase "This is going to hurt me more than it does you" came home to roost. All I could do was simply wrap my arms around my little boy and hold him.

After a few seconds, I explained to Will the best way I knew how why the memories we'd built during the past two weeks of adventure were more than any whitetail trophy we could put our hands on. The time we'd spent in the blind that morning, as well as the days leading up to it, had been so special. Trophies fade and gather dust, but our memories will be held in our hearts until our Lord and Savior, Jesus, calls us home.

Eventually the tears stopped and a boyish smile returned to my son's face. We slowly gathered up all the gear it takes to bag a deer and create videos of our time together. The walk back to the truck was long and quiet. It seemed to take much longer than it had when we'd left our parking spot, in the dark hours of the morning, filled with eager anticipation as we traveled to our favorite hunting ground. I'm sure some of the same thoughts were running through our heads now, but neither of us said anything. We just enjoyed the camaraderie together and reflected on all that we'd been blessed to experience during this special day and great time of hunting together in God's great outdoors.

Two years later, on November 14, at 5:19 in the evening, Will squeezed off a shot and claimed his first whitetail! It was a big, mature doe that field dressed out at 135 pounds.

As we were following the blood trail to recover the deer, I noticed her white belly ahead of us first. "Hey, Will! What's that up there by the tree line?"

Will looked up. When he saw the sizable doe, he took off running across the field whooping, hollering, and swinging his arms the entire way. My heart warms every time I think about that moment. His celebration was my trophy. All the work, time, and effort Will put into making that first harvest taught both of us so much and drew us closer together.

Over the past several seasons, Will and I have experienced the highs and lows that come with chasing wild game. The lows are plentiful. A few to mention are the ache of missed shots; the sick feeling of an unrecovered, wounded animal; an illness that keeps a hunter in bed on opening day of deer season; and arrows that jump off the rest in the middle of pulling a string to full draw. These types of disappointments can wreak havoc on the quality of a hunting season.

However, the highs of hunting have a way of erasing the effect of the lows. A few of the apex hunting moments with my son include, of course, watching him get his first deer, seeing him effectively apply the skills of following a blood trail that I'd taught him, being present and filming as he took his first turkey, and hearing his thoughtful thanks for taking him hunting. These mountaintop moments are special, to say the least, but there's one other that I hold very dear to my heart.

A most treasured "take away" from my experiences with my son is a thought that came to me while I was watching him enjoy a day in our hunting blind. As I observed his excited expression and his anticipation of a game sighting, I felt a love well up inside that was profound and deep. Suddenly I thought of the fact that I too was being watched. My Father in heaven was observing me in the same way I was watching my son. And it occurred to me that God loves me even more than I could ever love my son. And God is a Father who is not untouched by the things in life that affect His children.

When I see my kids hurt in any way, I hurt with them. When my children successfully accomplish new goals, such as harvesting a deer, turkey, squirrel or achieving something they've been working hard for in school, I rejoice with them. I realized that if I, a frail human, a "father who is not in heaven," could sense this depth of love for my children, how much more must the one who created everything love me as His child.

With that revelation as my motivation, that day I started making an effort to look at my life—my sweet wife, my children, my work, and my dreams—through my Father's eyes. This changed my perspective in drastic ways. I've found I'm more patient with people, especially family members. I'm more aware of the importance of not returning evil for evil but to give a blessing instead. I'm more ready to forgive and more willing to lend a hand. And I'm quicker to sacrifice my alone time in the deer woods so I can spend it with those I love and experience God's great outdoors together.

I'd like to be able to say I'm batting a thousand when it comes to successfully looking through my heavenly Father's eyes and acting as He would 100 percent of the time. However, that wouldn't be anywhere near true. But that is my goal, and I'm working hard at it. Because of that, I feel much better about who I am today. Furthermore, I have no plans of stopping my efforts at improving. Why? Because wherever I am, whether pressing my way through a thicket, flying an airplane (that's what I do for a living), resting in my living room, or sitting in a church pew, I know that just as I watched my son that day in the deer blind, God is watching me. And just as Will brought great joy to my heart as I looked at him, I want God to feel that way about me.

9

What Matters Most

by Charles J. Alsheimer

As Aaron ran toward me, he excitedly yelled, "Dad! Dad! I got one! I got a deer!" When he got to me, he continued. "Boy, Dad, it was something. Two does walked by my stand, and I shot one when it stopped about 10 yards from me. I made a perfect shot through both lungs."

Listening to his story caused a rush of emotion. I got as excited as he was. Before he could go on, I asked, "Well, where is she?"

"She ran about 75 yards before going down just above the creek."

I put my arm around his shoulder. "This is something you'll remember the rest of your life. You know, I was 30 when I killed my first deer with a bow and arrow. And you've done it at 15! Let's go get her."

Upon reaching the doe, we relived Aaron's moment again before field dressing her. Though he'd watched me go through the process many times, this one was special. Slowly, I went through each step and explained why and how I was doing it. We paused at one point to open the stomach to see what the doe had been eating. Then I cut through the diaphragm to remove the heart and lungs. As we studied the way the broadhead had sliced the lungs, I explained why the hit was so lethal. With the field dressing complete, I looked at Aaron as he ran his fingers through the doe's fur.

He looked up at me and said, "Boy, Dad, this deer is a blessing from God."

We then loaded the deer onto our tractor and headed for the house. Aaron was on cloud 9, and I was on cloud 10. As we rode down the hill toward home, my mind wandered back through the years. I thought back to the first deer I'd killed when I was 17. I remembered what had led to that important moment. That time was a high point in my life journey... a journey pieced together with hopes, plans, pains, and dreams.

Chasing the Dream

I was raised on a potato farm in the heart of New York's Finger Lakes region. My dad enjoyed deer hunting, though he wasn't extremely passionate about it. This was partly because he started taking me along when I was a mere five years old. I was a hyperactive kid, and I often drove him nuts in the woods with my tendency to be in constant motion—a trait not friendly at all to being on a deer stand. In spite of this, he continued to take me with him. We were buddies. Regardless of the challenges he faced in dealing with my hyper nature, he still wanted me with him.

Becoming a hunter was, without question, one thing that altered the course of my life, but nothing compares to how my life was changed on April 23, 1971. That was the day I accepted Jesus Christ as my Lord and Savior. Though I didn't know where my walk with God would take me, I was committed to following His plan for me. Little did I know that my Creator had designs for the two things I considered most important: following Him and hunting. He would use these to cut my trail for my time here on earth.

Along with growing in my walk with Christ and being an avid fan of the hunt, I also graduated from college. This accomplishment resulted in my immersion in the business world, but I never, for a moment, abandoned my intense interest in anything that pertained to hunting and all it entails.

To feed my interest in the outdoors, my wife, Carla, and I bought the property that bordered the farm I'd grown up on. We promptly turned it into a wildlife sanctuary. Then, after five years of marriage, my life completely changed again when God blessed us with our only child. As it turned out, my sweet wife had given birth to my very best hunting buddy! We named him Aaron.

Once Aaron was old enough to sit up and crawl, I took him with me everywhere on our farm. If I went scouting for deer on a warm summer evening, he went along. If I went someplace to photograph deer, he went along. He loved it. On more than one occasion, my childhood flashed before me as I sat with Aaron in the woods. As though zero years had passed, I saw myself sitting with my dad back on the home farm. The feelings were warm and precious as the memories of my time with him flooded my heart.

When Aaron was nearly two, Carla returned to teaching. At the same time, I made a major career decision that was motivated by my unbridled passion for hunting. I resigned my position in corporate sales and marketing to pursue a full-time career as a nature photographer, outdoor writer, and guest lecturer. It was an option that probably should have frightened me to the core. To be quite honest, though, I was so ready to do something with my time that utilized my real interests that it was not that difficult a choice to make. What little amount of apprehension that came with such a drastic course change was squelched by the support of my wife, as well as an assurance in my heart that it was simply the right thing to do. Though I wasn't sure how successful I would be at the new venture, I made the leap out of the business world and back into the wild.

Rather than hire a babysitter, Carla and I decided Aaron would spend his days with me. Until he started school, my son tagged along with me to hunting blinds, waterfowl and deer photography shoots, and public lectures. We became known as the "whitetail guy and his kid." Needless to say, we had some interesting times together that caused us to bond strongly as father and son. One of the more memorable moments we had took place a long way from our New York home. In fact, it was way out West in the Rocky Mountains.

Nature photography took the two of us to some of the most incredible places on earth. In the early 1980s, while on a working vacation in the Wyoming Rockies, four-year-old Aaron and I hiked to the top of Yellowstone's Mount Washburn for a day of photographing bighorn sheep. Upon reaching the summit, we located a herd. I began feverishly taking shot after shot as the sheep grazed on alpine grasses.

All the time I was looking through my camera's viewfinder, Aaron was focusing on something far more magnificent—the hundreds of miles of wilderness that stretched out below us. As my camera's motor drive whirred, I felt Aaron's little hand tugging on my coat. I ignored him and kept on shooting. Moments later I felt a second, firmer tug, and I realized

I'd better see what he wanted. Without taking my eyes off the sheep, I softly asked, "Yes, what is it?"

In a whisper he replied, "Dad, didn't God make us a beautiful world?"

I stopped taking pictures and put the camera down. I wrapped my arm around his little shoulders as we gazed at the panorama before us. While I was trying to get the next, great, prize-winning bighorn sheep photo, my son "got it" because he saw the bigger picture. He was worshiping the God who made everything he was admiring. I realized that day that my love for the two things that had captured my attention from boyhood on up—God and His marvelous outdoors—had been successfully passed down to my son.

Aaron and I left the Wyoming mountain that day with a lot more than just a bag filled with rolls of film that were hopefully packed with outdoor photos to help put food on our table. We also left with a worship memory that I've never forgotten. Aaron hasn't either.

The Blessing

Space doesn't allow me to share what the last 30 years have been like, but suffice it to say it's been incredible—a blessing from God. I was privileged to lead Aaron to the Lord when he was eight. Through the years we've spent a lot of time together traveling, photographing, and hunting some of the most beautiful places in North America. As great as these adventures have been, few things have been able to top the times we've shared hunting turkeys and whitetails on our farm. A memorable hunt from 10 years ago captures our hunting bond.

It was Sunday, October 22, a great day in western New York. It dawned clear and cold, the kind of day every bowhunter dreams of. After going to church with Carla and Aaron, we celebrated his birthday. It seemed hard to believe that he was now a man in his twenties. From the time I'd awoken that morning, my mind had been drifting to the memories we'd shared since he came into the world. In a little more than 20 unbelievably short years, he'd gone from being a little tyke following me around in the woods to a 6'3" giant of a man (physically and spiritually) now involved in the corporate world.

After an early afternoon dinner, Aaron said, "Dad, what do you say we end the day in a deer stand?" Because of his career path, this was the first time we'd bowhunted together in a long time, so I jumped at the opportunity like a chicken on a June bug. A couple hours before sundown, we headed to our favorite haunts on our farm. The temperature had risen to 60 degrees, so I didn't expect much action. Even so, hunting together and seeing the sunset from a deer stand would be more than enough.

The first hour was slow as I'd suspected it would be. We did see a few squirrels darting around in the woods. Then, with about an hour of daylight left, a doe and two fawns passed under my stand before entering a nearby food plot. Within minutes, an eight-point buck slipped through the hardwoods and into the plot. During the next 45 minutes, three yearling bucks appeared to fill their bellies, along with 19 turkeys. It was quite a sight to see the bucks, does, and turkeys feeding in the same field at the same time.

With no interest in killing any of the bucks, I studied the turkeys through my binoculars as they walked in Aaron's direction. Above us, in the New York sky, there were crisscrossing jet trails and cirrus clouds that began to turn amber from the sun's rays as it inched toward the horizon. With no air movement whatsoever, I could actually hear a doe munching on clover as legal shooting time ended. I slipped my arrow into the bow's quiver and sat motionless for several minutes before climbing down from the stand. I wanted to treasure the scene as long as I could.

After gathering up my equipment, I crossed the food plot to pick up Aaron. He was at the base of his tree waiting for me. When I got to him I whispered, "What did you see?"

He responded, "Boy, what a day! That was a great sit."

"Well, what did you see?" I repeated.

He replied, "Oh, just a couple does, 19 turkeys, and a great sunset."

"No bucks?" I asked.

In one motion he swung his arm around my neck and shoulder and hugged me before saying, "No, just God's handiwork. That and a chance to hunt again with you is more than enough."

I was speechless. My eyes watered as I stared into my son's eyes less than two feet away. His affection and words tugged at my heart the way his four-year-old hand had tugged on my coat back on that Wyoming mountain many years earlier. It was a special moment filled with happiness and sadness. I was happy because of the tender words I'd just heard my son say to me. It was also a little sad that, because of the cares of life, moments like the one we'd just had were becoming fewer and further between.

Because I'd often used Aaron as a model in the hunting scenes I'd photographed, the readers of *Deer and Deer Hunting* magazine (and other outdoor publications that have printed my writings and photos) saw him grow up through the years. But what the readers can't see is just how deep the bond is between the two of us. I explain the blessing he's been in a special way. It is best worded in John 10:10. The Lord Jesus said, "I have come that they may have life, and have it to the full" (NIV). I can testify that God certainly kept that promise with me. He not only saved me, but He heaped joy upon me by giving me the blessing of my son. I can also say that Aaron's and my immense love for each other has been cultivated through the years by our mutual passion for being together in God's marvelous creation.

If you have a son or sons, and if you hunt with them, my prayer for you first is that you will give your life to the God who gives only good gifts, including children. Along with that, I pray that you will lead your offspring to walk with Him. I also pray that together you will enjoy the trail of this life just as Aaron and I do. If these things happen to you, my friend, you have truly found what matters most!

10

Mountaineer Memories

by Steve Chapman with George Ferrell

One of the most interesting song titles I've ever heard is "I Don't Like Half the Folks I Love." It's amazing how so few words can imply so much. It's my understanding that the songwriter thought of the "hook" and penned the lyrics after going to a family reunion. I can't help but wonder if he left the event beat up and scarred emotionally and/or physically. For whatever reason the song was written, I'm very happy to report that as a songwriter it isn't a title I would have come up with because it doesn't fit anyone in the Chapman family, immediate or extended.

A Chapman family reunion always takes place in the town of Chapmanville, West Virginia. Yep, you read it right. The town is named after my family. The gathering is invariably fun. Besides a yard full of delightful relatives to connect with who come from various parts of the country, there is plenty of well-cooked food and some newborn Chapmans to dote over. There is also lots of singing and some of the best clean joke telling on the planet.

All these great features make our reunions memorable occasions. But there is one more I have to add that, in years past, has made the gathering even more of a treat. It's seeing the gleam in the eyes of my Uncle Jimmy. Jimmy Ferrell was married to my dad's sister, Daisy. At our gatherings, he'd talk about going hunting with his son, George, and his grandson, Travis. Sadly, Jimmy's face won't be in the pictures that will be taken at future reunions. His passing and absence will leave quite a void in the group shot, but we have our memories of him to enjoy.

As I considered the dads I wanted to invite to contribute to this book, I thought of my cousin George. I figured he could provide memorable tales of being with Uncle Jimmy in the hunter's woods. Not only did I want to honor the memory of my uncle by including him, but I was also eager to hear the stories dear to my cousin's heart. I hope you enjoy these tales based on one deer hunt George went on with his dad.

The Bobcat

My first deer hunting trip with Dad was when I was a 19 years old, just prior to my going into the Air Force. We went to the big mountains of Pendleton County, where Dad had hunted for several seasons with his buddies. On the Saturday before opening day on Monday, we were biding our time by squirrel hunting. As I sat under a huge oak waiting for a bushy-tail to show itself, I spotted a bobcat quietly sneaking through the timber. I had a Winchester Model 37, 20-gauge, "poke stock" shotgun. I managed to move around and take a shot. The bobcat dropped in its tracks.

When I got back to camp with the cat and told the story, Dad listened with a big smile. I'll never forget how good it felt to hear him tell me how proud he was that I was able to maintain enough composure to outsmart the eyes of such an intelligent animal, as well as let it get close enough to get the job done with a short-range scattergun. As a 19-year-old who was about to leave home to do military duty, I needed the boost in self-confidence Dad provided that day. I carried his encouragement with me into the Air Force and, actually, into the rest of my life.

The "Ten" That Got Away

I didn't have my own hunting rifle for deer season, so for my first experience at chasing West Virginia whitetails, Dad borrowed a Model .30-30 Winchester from his brother for me to use. I loved the feel of Uncle David's gun, and I cradled it in my arms like I would a newborn puppy as we left camp on opening day. The November weather was clear but bitterly cold. Dad and I split up to find our places to watch for deer.

For a reason I can't explain other than feeling it would be best to be elevated as I watched the woods, I picked a large pine tree to sit in. It turned out to be a bad idea! Sitting up on a pine branch like a roosted turkey in frigid winter weather isn't an ideal place for anyone to be, especially a newbie deer hunter like I was. Being high enough to be exposed to biting wind made it doubly difficult to sit still and feel secure and safe. Still, I stuck to my pine perch and waited for daylight to come.

It wasn't long after daybreak that I saw a deer walking along the ridge some 300 yards from where I sat. I remember two distinct feelings as the deer wandered out of range. My body felt frozen on the outside, but inside I was totally fired up by the sight of a deer. What happened next surprised me. I shivered uncontrollably. I couldn't tell if it was the cold on my skin or the deer in my vision that was causing it. Experience has since taught me that either one can start a fellow shaking, but I didn't know at the time that seeing a deer could cause the onset of a bone-rattling condition veteran hunters refer to as "buck fever." All I knew was that I couldn't hold still.

The relentless shivering didn't serve me well with what happened a little while later either. As I fought not to shake, I heard something that sounded like footsteps coming from my right. I couldn't believe my eyes when I saw a nice 10-point approaching. The sight kicked my nervousness into high gear, and my body shook so much I had to concentrate to stay seated on the pine branch. My dad's words came to me in the midst of the mental chaos. "Be calm, breathe deep, don't get too excited." I could almost hear his voice as the words filled my head. I wondered what he'd think if he could hear my thoughts as I responded to the echo of his coaching: "Yeah, right. What a load of crock that is!" I figured I was doing well to remember to draw my next breath, much less think about staying calm, cool, and collected. I'm sure the entire pine tree was shaking by then, and the gun felt like it weighed 100 pounds.

To this day I can't explain how I managed to move the .30-30 around to rest it on a limb, how I took aim at the big buck, and how I pulled the trigger. My first-ever shot at a deer was dead on! I whispered, "Bull's-eye!" Man, was I wrong. The deer raised his head up, and without a moment's hesitation took off like the wind. I worked the lever like "the Rifleman" did on the old 1960's TV show. Using the buck's white-furred butt as a target, I took a second shot, a third, and then a fourth. I seriously thought, *How can an animal keep running with that many holes in it?*

Suddenly the buck stopped and stared back in my direction. I had one more round to throw at him but, lo and behold, my gun jammed. I frantically tried to unjam the action, constantly looking back and forth from the gun to the deer, from the deer to the gun. The deer remained standing in the woods about 250 yards away. I finally removed the stuck cartridge and loaded a couple of shells into the magazine. I hurriedly rested the barrel on a nearby limb. I aimed and fired one more shot. The leaves flew up under the buck's belly. With that, he ran over the ridge and out of sight.

I immediately came down from my perch. Within a minute or two I found drops of blood in the leaves. It wasn't much, but I followed what little I could find in the thick laurel. As I tried to guess where the next evidence of my wounded deer would be, a shot rang out just down the hill from me. It didn't require a lot of deer-hunting experience to know what had happened. Though I didn't want to face the reality, I was sure the buck had escaped me and gotten into the sights of another hunter's gun. As it turned out, I was sadly right.

I stood there on the mountainside for a while, hoping against hope that the 10-point might have dodged the other bullet and decided to come back up the hill. But it didn't happen. I faced the music and headed back to camp. Dad was there already. When he saw me, he could see right away how disappointed I was. He told me he'd heard the shooting, and he just knew I'd killed my first deer. Like a good friend, he listened as I told the details of what had happened. When he learned that the big buck had likely yielded bragging rights for another hunter, he offered some reality by schooling me on one of the most important-but-unwritten laws of the deer woods.

"George, whoever brings the deer down gets to put the tag on it. It's just the way it is. It might not feel fair, but keep in mind that someday you might be on the receiving end of the deal. If so, you'll have more compassion on the guy who sent the deer to you because today you sent a deer to another hunter."

Learning that law didn't lessen the disappointment I was feeling, but what did help tremendously was simply talking to Dad about it. I've heard it said that "with a true friend, joys are doubled and sorrows are halved." That day I learned how accurate that statement is. Telling Dad how hard it was to have been so close to getting a trophy but losing it made the painful weight of loss feel much lighter.

While I returned to the woods and hunted that evening, Dad went over to another camp to visit a couple of old buddies he'd hunted with through the years. He told them what had happened and described the location where I'd taken the shots. His friends informed him that a 10-point was hanging in the next camp down. His buddies reported that the fellow who'd killed the massive animal heard a noise in the brush and shot into it. (That riled Dad pretty good since it was such a foolish and unsafe thing to do.) They'd heard the guy's deer already had a few holes in it when it was taken down.

When Dad gave me that news later that evening, he was patient as he heard me rant about the outcome of the day. Then he calmly talked me off the ledge of depression and back into a willingness to get up the next day to try again. He was always good at doing that kind of thing for me.

The Blessed Bullet

On the same hunting trip where I got the bobcat and lost the 10-point, I learned an even greater lesson. As if enough hadn't already happened to talk about for the rest of our years together, later that evening in the camper Dad had an opportunity to teach me something that had life-saving potential. After watching me clean the exterior of Uncle Dave's .30-30, he offered me some advice.

"George, one of the most dangerous things a man can ever do is clean a gun. You just never know what might be in it."

As he spoke, I worked the lever and pulled the trigger to prove that I was cleaning an empty gun. Thankfully the gun was pointing toward an uninhabited area. Dad flinched. After making sure I understood how mindless it was to drop the hammer of a weapon while inside and without checking the chamber, he talked to me about how incredibly important it is to make safety the top priority of hunting. I apologized for putting us at risk and worked the lever again to do some cleaning inside the chamber. When I did, much to my surprise and Dad's, out popped an unexpended cartridge.

I immediately realized what I'd done. I'd failed to remember the two extra rounds I'd loaded that morning after shooting at the buck. I had used only one of the two, and the lone bullet was still in the gun when I'd reloaded and went back to hunt that evening. When I got back to the camper, I thought I'd ejected all the shells before going inside, but I hadn't. It could have been a deadly oversight.

When the cartridge came tumbling out, Dad instantly sat up straight in his chair, his back stiff and his eyes wide. I sat motionless as the shell bounced on the linoleum floor. My heart beat like the thumping of a kick drum. Finally Dad leaned over and picked up the bullet. As he turned it in his fingers and looked at it closely, he turned a strange shade of pale. Without saying a word, he turned it around and showed me the bottom of the cartridge. What I saw made my blood run cold. The primer had a dent from the firing pin when I'd pulled the trigger a few minutes before. Thankfully the shell hadn't fired.

We both knew one of us could have died that evening or, at the least, both of us could have lost our hearing. We had no one to thank but God in heaven for protecting us from such a disaster. Dad kept the shell for two reasons. He used it as a very effective way of illustrating to his grandkids just how dangerous using and cleaning a gun can be, and he kept it as evidence that sometimes supernatural intervention is required to shelter us from harm.

Success at Last

We hunted Tuesday but didn't see anything. Wednesday started the same as Monday. I figured since the pine tree had yielded some action, I would visit it again. This time, however, I had a different gun. I figured if a .30-30 couldn't close the deal, a 12-gauge shotgun with a heavy "punkin' ball" would do it. Dad had suggested his old, dependable, slick-barrel gun. He said that if I used it at a close enough distance, it would provide all the knockdown power needed. About 10 o'clock that morning I put his claim to the test.

One of our friends shot at a six-point higher up on the ridge, and after the report of his gun all I could hear was crashing as something came down the ridge through the timber toward me. All of a sudden a deer jumped over what appeared to be a 10-foot-high laurel and headed straight toward me. It passed close enough I could almost see the whiskers on its nose.

From my pine limb location, all I had time to do was swing the gun like a pistol from one side of the branch I was sitting on to the other. I finally took desperate aim and pulled the trigger. I found out that a 12-gauge takes meat on both ends of the gun because my shoulder nearly broke with the heavy recoil of the stock. But that wasn't half the damage that the punkin' ball did to the deer. The bullet sent the buck down to his knees. I pumped another shell in and braced myself for the evil that my shoulder was about to endure and pulled the trigger again. The second shot found the deer's neck, and the deed was done.

I climbed down out of the pine tree faster than lightning and ran over to the lifeless prize. Without concern for anyone else hunting on the mountain, I let out a victory whoop that probably still echoes there today. Dad was near enough to hear my yelling and hollered back to let me know that he knew what had happened. He told me later how big he smiled when the sound of my celebration reached his ears. He mentioned what a chuckle he got out of assuming the rest of West Virginia had heard it as well.

More than once through the years I reminded Dad that I took more off the mountain that week than just my first deer. From feeling the strength in his affirmation after I took the wily bobcat to learning to embrace the unwritten "law of hunting" after the big ten-pointer got away, from seeing the evidence of God's protection in the dented primer of the .30-30 shell to achieving success in the field, our game bag was full of tales to pass on to family, especially grandkids and great-grandkids, and friends.

Needless to say, I miss Dad more than words can tell, but never more than when the opening day of hunting season comes in West Virginia. The old camper just doesn't feel the same without him in it with us.

The Hunt Is Over

Daddy's old truck, smell of coffee in his cup,
And how the highway seemed so empty at four a.m.
These are things I remember as we headed to the timber.
We were off to chase the whitetails again.

With Dad on a Deer Stand

Cold November stand, golden sunrise on the land,
And how the big ones could appear just like a ghost.
The sun going down, that's when I'd hear the sound,
Of Daddy's words he knew I dreaded most...

It's time to go, the hunt is over.
Throw that old Winchester gun across your shoulder.
I know it's been good, son, to be here in these woods,
But it's time to go on home.
The hunt is over.

When I got my first deer I thought I saw a tear
Running down that smile on Daddy's face.
He said, "You might pull the trigger someday on something bigger,
But, son, this is one you can't replace."

He lived for the seasons, and I lived for the reasons
He would take me back up to those hills again.
Just to be up there together, thought these times would last forever,
But today the good Lord said to him...

"It's time to go, the hunt is over.
Throw that old Winchester gun across your shoulder.
I know it's been good, son, to be here in these woods,
But it's time to come on home.
The hunt is over."[1]

11

Ain't Nothin' Like the Last One

by Steve Chapman

Standing at around 6'4", Jeff was a mountain of a man with broad shoulders, thick neck, and a bushy, red beard. His massive hands seemed permanently stained by his work as a Pennsylvania farmer. His boots were well worn and held the evidence that he'd likely come straight from the barn to the church where I was to speak at a wild game dinner that evening. As Jeff was telling me a few details about himself, the event sponsor came up, put his arm over Jeff's shoulder, and said to me, "Glad the two of you are getting to know each other already 'cause we're going over to this man's place tomorrow morning for breakfast before you head back to Tennessee."

At daybreak the next day we were pulling into a long, gravel driveway that led to a little brick structure sitting at the base of a tall hill. The sponsor could tell I was a little puzzled about the site of the building since it didn't look like someone's home. It looked more like a clubhouse.

"This is not where Jeff lives," he explained. "He lives on down the road in a huge, old farmhouse. This is the place he and his family and friends gather to deer hunt. This old, brick house holds a lot of memories. I'm grateful to be on the list of the guys that headquarter here during our rifle season."

On the metal door of the building was a sign that read "Hunters Only." I felt right at home as we walked in. Once inside, the smell of sausage, eggs, biscuits, and coffee permeated the air, along with the wonderful aroma of the firewood that crackled in the freestanding, potbellied stove.

There were a couple of six-foot, homemade, cafeteria-type tables placed in the center of the room, where a dozen or so men were sitting. They turned to greet us, the expressions on their faces relaxed and welcoming. It was easy to see the camaraderie they enjoyed with one another was something they cherished as much as they valued the air they breathed. It was a delightful gathering of like-minded men, the kind of group most die-hard hunters would enjoy being part of.

The humor among the men was especially infectious. It seemed that each one had a joke to tell that they'd just heard. One of my favorites was the story a younger fellow told that he'd gotten from an email.

> Seems there was a wife who texted her husband and said, "Windows frozen. What to do?"
>
> The husband texted back, "Pour warm water."
>
> The wife texted back a few minutes later. "Now the whole computer is messed up!"

The noise that erupted was music to my ears. Hardly anything is as pleasing as the sound of a group of men enjoying a good laugh. After a few more well-told tales, it was time to chow down on the feast that had been prepared by the camp cook. Everyone quieted down, one of the fellows led us in thankful applause for the chef (who was a mechanic by trade), another gentleman offered a prayer of thanksgiving for the food, and following a concert of "Amens" we started stabbing at our vittles with our forks and knives like a group of barbarians.

I sat across the table from the game dinner sponsor and Jeff. Jeff's stature, even while sitting, was impressive. I remembered that I'd looked up at him when we talked, but I hadn't felt the least bit intimidated by his presence. I didn't know just how gentle such a large fellow could be until the event sponsor brought up a detail that made Jeff's shoulders fall a little.

"There's someone not with us today at this camp house, and we all miss him terribly."

Though the room was filled with the sound of guys talking to each other, I noticed that things suddenly started to quiet as the sponsor continued.

"Jeff's dad was the heartbeat of this place. Actually, this camp was his brainchild, and a bunch of us pitched in and put bricks and mortar on his idea. He did everything from cook to cut wood, from shuttling hunters to their stands to skinning their deer for them. Bill was the best friend any of us had. And then the thief showed up."

I had a feeling I knew who the thief was. My suspicions were confirmed when the sponsor went on.

"Jeff, I know it might not be easy to do, but would you honor your dad by telling our guest a little about him and his fight with Alzheimer's? Especially what he said to you during last year's deer season."

Jeff shifted in his chair a bit, looked toward the door, and just stared quietly for a few seconds. By now the room was as quiet as a windless morning in the deep woods. He choked up a little as he started talking.

"Only God in heaven knows how much I wish that door would open right now and I'd see my dad walk through it. He was the best. I was only nine years old when he took me deer hunting for the first time. Mom protested that first hunt—said I was way too young, but she knew it was a battle she wouldn't win.

"I didn't carry a gun that first time out. I just sat and watched a man watch the woods. Some kids might have been bored silly sitting there in the cold like I did that day, but for some reason I didn't find it boring at all. Maybe it was the intense look on Dad's face as he scanned the area that intrigued me. Maybe it was the sight of the Winchester .30-30 that seemed so huge and powerful. Or maybe it was just being there next to someone I felt so safe with. Maybe it was all of these, but for whatever reason, I was hooked. I could feel it."

Jeff looked toward the potbellied stove and pointed. "That old stove was in our house where I grew up—and where I still live. I can remember getting dressed by it with Dad on opening day of the next season. This time, at ten years old, I would be pulling the trigger if we saw something. I can still feel the excitement that ran through me as we headed out the front door and walked toward the hill where we'd spend the morning together."

The story of Jeff's first experience as a hunter with his dad held my attention. He described the action he hadn't forgotten, and probably never would.

"Our Pennsylvania winters can be brutal at times, and that first hunt with a real live gun in my hand wasn't made any easier by temperatures that dipped to somewhere around 20 degrees. Thankfully, I remember the air was dead still. Dad commented how fortunate we were to not be beaten up by a bitter wind. We both sat on five-gallon buckets with our backs to the sun as it rose and began to warm us a little. My feet felt like ice cubes, but I fought to not move them around. Dad mentioned how impressed he was that I was able to sit still. That made me want to sit even 'stiller.' Finally, around 8:30, after sitting there nearly two hours, Dad nudged me. Without saying a word, he slowly pointed down the hill toward the big pond we sat above. I saw the movement he'd seen, and for a moment I totally forgot about how cold I was. And then something happened that I couldn't explain, but Dad knew."

I had an educated guess at what had happened to Jeff and should have waited for him to reveal it, but I was so engaged in the story that I couldn't hold it back. "Let me guess. It's the same thing that happens to us all when our body core gets cool and then we're hit by a rush of deer fever. We start trembling uncontrollably. I bet you could hardly pick the gun up out of your lap."

Jeff smiled. "You've been there, huh?" he commented.

"Sure have, man. Been there and suffered through that. But why would we go hunting if it weren't that exciting?"

Jeff heartily agreed and cupped his hand around his coffee mug as he went on. "Dad forced himself not to laugh as I raised the heavy rifle and tried keeping it steady enough to aim with the open sights. The doe that had walked within 50 yards or so of us stood broadside while looking down the hill. She didn't know we were there. Dad gently patted me on the leg and whispered, 'Son, take a deep breath and try not to have a cardiac.'"

I chuckled as I imagined a young Jeff trying to get a grip on his emotions while on the deer stand.

"Well..." Jeff paused and laughed. "I had no idea what he meant by *cardiac*, but I did know he was trying to coach me through my battle with the shakes. After a few seconds of trying everything I could to get a bead on the doe, I gave up and asked Dad for some help. When I did, he quietly slipped off his bucket and went onto all fours in front of me, his back under my rifle. I rested my elbows on his ribs. He whispered, 'If you're on her good, pull the hammer back and take the shot.' I followed orders, felt like I had a good hold on the sights, and pulled the trigger."

Everyone in the room had probably heard the story more than once, but they acted like they were hearing it for the first time like I was.

"Please tell me your shot was good!" someone called out.

Jeff's chin rose a little. "Yep! She dropped right where she stood. Dad couldn't have been a happier man, and I couldn't have been more surprised. He said, 'Boy, ain't nothin' like the first one.' He was so right."

I could see Jeff's eyes beginning to water. It was a little odd to see the combination of tears and a man of such stature, but in reality it takes a lot of strength to cry, especially in front of a group of men. But Jeff needed it in that moment. The sight made me like him even more.

"Sounds like you and your dad were close," I commented.

Jeff took a deep breath. "We were indeed. We hunted together every year from then on. I was a teenager when he got the idea for this camp house. It became *the* place for family and friends to congregate during hunting season. Though it's not that pretty, I wouldn't take a million dollars for it. It has Dad written all over it. "

My host spoke up and asked Jeff to tell me what his dad had said the previous season. Jeff seemed a little reluctant. I took it as a sign that it was probably not an easy thing to share.

"Dad contracted Alzheimer's Disease about five years ago," Jeff finally said. "As he got progressively worse, he seemed to get more agitated and harder to predict. He especially dreaded deer season early on in the battle because he knew he wouldn't be permitted to run around our hills with a rifle in his hands. He didn't like sitting at home while the rest of us went deer hunting. We tried to console him with our stories and pictures, but it didn't make him feel that much better about it."

I felt bad for the man who sat across from me as he struggled to keep his chin from quivering. The part of his story that came next was unforgettable.

"Dad lived with me and my wife during the latter part of his fight with Alzheimer's. As the symptoms advanced, we noticed from time to time that he would drift in and out of an awareness of reality. So last season I told my brothers and sisters that if I detected that he was in one of those times when he seemed alert, I wanted to take him hunting with me. Sure enough, around the second week of the season he perked up. I woke him up one morning and invited him to go with me. He smiled and agreed to go. I helped him get dressed in some of his old camo, and we headed to the woods."

I looked around at the guys in the room, and they were quietly waiting for the rest of the story. They knew what was coming.

"I didn't take him out before daylight. The day was too cold. I waited until about an hour after sunrise so walking would be easier and to let the temperature get up a little. Just like we did when I was a kid, we took our seats on our five-gallon buckets. Dad had lost a good bit of weight and looked a little like a 10-year-old with his loose-fitting clothes and his old hat that came way down over his forehead. I couldn't look at him very long without wanting to burst out in tears. We sat there for about an hour, and lo and behold, across the hill I heard the familiar sound of running deer. A small herd dropped down in the ravine below us and started up the hill toward where we were sitting."

"Did your dad know what was happening?" I asked.

Jeff lightly slapped the table with the palm of a big hand and smiled. "Amazingly he did. He flinched a bit when the sound of their hooves crashing in the dry leaves reached his ears. He said, 'Well, looky there!' I figured since he knew what was headed up the hill, it was time to hand the rifle to him. He took it like he knew what he was doing. He bent forward and rested his elbows on his knees with the gun pointing downhill. When a large doe presented herself at about 60 yards, Dad looked through the scope, cleared his throat as if he were a little nervous, pulled the hammer back, and dropped it on the firing pin. That doe never knew what hit her."

The smile that came over my face was as big as the ones on everybody's face. "That is so cool!" I exclaimed. "Who would've ever thought your dad would have the wherewithal to not only get the shot off but to put it in the right spot. That's great!"

Jeff smiled big too as he continued. "I said, 'Dad, from what I can tell, getting this deer was as exciting for you as your first one!' He grinned from ear-to-ear and shook his head as if he couldn't believe what had just happened. He wasn't too familiar with what a high-five was, but I raised my hand and coached him through it. Men in his day simply shook hands, so we did that too.

"That's when he got really quiet. I was afraid his mind was going back behind the wall of the illness, but that's not what was happening at all. Instead, for almost a half-minute, he sat and looked down the hill at the deer he'd taken. Finally he broke the silence with words that will be forever etched in my mind. 'Son, the first one was definitely a thrill, but I'm tellin' you now, ain't nothin' like the last one.'"

A quiet hush came over the room and lingered. All I could do was look down at the table and hope I could keep from falling apart. I can't remember when a statement jolted me like that one. I'd just heard some of the most heartrending words I believe I'd ever heard or will ever hear. I didn't say a thing. Actually, I couldn't say anything. I just sat there and waited for my soul to stop hurting.

Then Jeff continued.

"I can't tell you how grateful I am that we had that last hunt together. Dad was there when I got my first one; I was there when he got his last one. The son had become the dad, and the dad had become the son. The circle of life was drawn, and I couldn't do a thing about it. Our family told Dad good-bye earlier this year."

Then Jeff looked at me with eyes that were awash in tears and offered some wisdom that is good for every father, son, and daughter to hear.

"A lot of guys think that hunting is all about killing, and there was a time when I thought that way too. But not anymore. That one moment with Dad and me sitting side-by-side on those blaze-orange plastic buckets...and hearing what Dad said after he took his final deer...taught me that hunting is all about life, relationships, and making memories with people I love. That's how I want to hunt until my turn comes to say, 'Ain't nothin' like the last one!'"

12

The Season

by Tim Smith

The Time Had Come

The wise King Solomon once said, "There is a time for everything, and a season for every activity under the heavens" (Ecclesiastes 3:1 NIV). In my estimation, that sage ol' leader had to be a deer hunter who knew that the next season never comes in fast enough and it always goes out way too early. Furthermore, I'm quite certain this verse was his kingly way of easing the anxiety of all the deer hunters in Camp Jerusalem. He was saying, "Opening day is gonna get here soon enough, boys. I'm sure the drop-tine monster of your dreams will show himself for you. So just settle down."

While I can't, of course, vouch for the accuracy of my idea that King Solomon was a deer hunter, his wisdom is spot-on true for those of us who live and hunt. There really is "a season for every activity under the heavens," including taking deer. That reality meant something significant for my son, Zach, and me. This particular year was going to be his first attempt at bagging a whitetail, but because of the legal time frames we hunt, we had to wait...and wait...and then wait some more for the season to roll around. As a dad who looked forward to guiding his son to his first deer, it felt like time was taking forever for that opening day to come. To help me endure the waiting, I entertained the hopes that it would indeed be the year my youngster would join the "First One Club."

Zach had been a good student of the hunt. He'd been with me as an observer on several adventures in previous seasons. On each trip, he'd been very focused (as focused as a kid under the age of seven could be). Because Zach had been so hungry for deer-hunting knowledge, I was fully convinced that I'd passed on the "hunter gene" to him. On each trip afield, he asked a truckload of questions on topics ranging from deer tracks to deer antlers, from deer ears to deer hooves, from deer food to deer droppings, from...well, you get the point.

In and out of the stand he'd intently imitated each and every move I made. If I took a step a certain way, he took a step the same way. If I moved slowly, he moved slowly. If I looked through my binoculars, he wanted to look through my binoculars (he often saw animals I never did, including lions and grizzlies). His job as my apprentice was to carry the backpack and blow the grunt-call when the need arose and as directed. Lately I could tell the boy was ready for some new responsibilities, such as helping me move stands, clear shooting lanes, and mount trail cameras.

The desire to be a deer hunter was strong in him—so much so that his favorite television shows were no longer Sponge Bob and Scooby-Do. He became an avid fan of *Realtree Roadtrips* and *Primos Truth About Hunting*. The kid had an insatiable appetite for the hunt. Who was I to try to bridle this passion? When the season came, the reality was as clear as a cloudless morning sky. The kid was gonna hunt!

Prep Work

While I was happily feeding my son's quickly growing passion for all things deer hunting, his mother wasn't so convinced he was ready to make the transition from a boy with a pretend gun to a boy with a real gun. I made my case with her more than once by saying, "How can the boy be a real hunter if he doesn't have a real gun?" She would repel my well-worded hints that I wanted to get Zach a gun with a line that has been used by mothers everywhere, taken straight out of the movie *Christmas Story*: "But he'll shoot his eye out." In response, like a real man and husband would do, I let my woman know how it was gonna be. I told her in no uncertain terms that "the boy was gonna be totin' a killin' stick this season whether she liked it or not." Actually, as you can probably guess, I begged and pleaded with her, and after numerous long discussions, my wife conceded to letting me get a gun for Zach. As a result, on his eighth birthday,

Zachary Ty Smith received his first real gun. We named her LuLu. We thought a female name for the rifle would help settle his mama's nerves regarding her boy's new companion.

Within an hour or two after I made the presentation of LuLu, Zach and I took her to the range. LuLu was a Rossi .410. She fit Zach's chin and shoulder perfectly—not too long, not too heavy, not too light—just right. Zach embraced LuLu like a boy hugs a new little puppy. In turn, LuLu returned his tenderness by not excessively kicking back when he pulled her trigger. Right out of the box, the boy and his boom-maker were putting holes in small cans at 20 yards. (Zach was shooting slugs in preparation for deer season.) The practicing continued throughout the late summer and into the early fall. My "chip off the old block" was consistently layin' the smack down at the shooting range, and I was convinced he was ready. I just needed to put him on a deer. It was go time for my only begotten!

The Hunt

It was a perfect late-autumn afternoon in the Deep South. The wind was ideal for our setup over a food plot we'd planted in early September. God had blessed us with the necessary rain, and the field was plush with brassicas and winter wheat. The deer had been going to it like ants to a picnic table. I'd hunted this plot several times previously, so I knew the does would come into the field way before dark. This would give my soon-to-be deer slayer ample opportunity for a shot. I was as sure as the coming sunset that the hunt we were on that evening would be great for Zach. It was going to happen. My son was going to harvest his first deer.

I let Zach in on the game plan around lunchtime. As expected, he was absolutely stoked! He too was convinced it was his day for success. For the next couple of hours he prepared for the hunt. In his youthful and unbridled anticipation, by one o'clock he'd donned every camo item he owned and filled his field pack with every item he could stuff into it. An onlooker would have sworn we were going on a Yukon expedition by the number of things that little guy put in his pack. I figured this was his hunt, and if he wanted a cough suppressant, a Game Boy, a Snickers bar, 63 Jolly Ranchers, 3 Juicy Juices, 2 Hot Wheel cars, a set of binoculars, 8 hand warmers, and a grunt call in his pack, well, who was I to stop him? Between two and three that afternoon, Zach asked no less than 523 times if it was "go" time.

And 523 times I gently said, "No." His relentless inquiries might have been torture to some dads, but for me it was music to my ears.

Finally, around 3:15, I announced that it was go time. With LuLu on his shoulder and his pack strapped on his back, Zach joined me as we began the long, three-minute hike from our house to the enclosed, elevated stand. By 3:30, we were settled in and ready for action. Zach unpacked all the contents of his pack in the shooting house. He lined the items up on the floor by order of priority. If you're wondering which items took top billing, I can report that the Juicy Juice, binoculars, and LuLu were right up front, standing within his reach and ready for action. All the other items were against the back wall. With this arrangement as his chosen tactic, I could tell the kid was taking the opportunity very seriously.

Like clockwork, at 4:30 three large does appeared at the edge of the field.

I whispered to Zach, "Let's put our ear coverings on and get ready. This could be it!"

He too had seen the does and was sizing them up through his binoculars. At this point they were about 50 yards away. After getting an assessment of their sizes, he readied LuLu.

I slid the small Plexiglas window of the shooting house open and urged Zach to quietly and slowly slip LuLu's barrel out and get ready for a shot. Because we knew that his "dead-on accurate" shooting range was 20 yards, we had agreed in advance that he would take a shot at any legal deer that made its way within that distance. As if they were being pulled in with a string, all three deer made their way toward our stand.

The shooting house was as quiet as a burial tomb as the three deer stepped toward us. However, the closer they got, the more I noticed a sort of drumming sound. It was faint at first. I noted that its rhythm was steady, quick-paced, and constant. Bum bum…bum bum…bum bum. As the deer inched closer, the pounding got louder and faster. What was this strange sound? When the trio of females got to within 25 yards, I finally realized what the strange noise was. It was my little hunter's heart beating in *overdrive*.

As I took a close look at young Zach, he didn't look all that good. He had a blank expression on his face, and it looked like a lightning bolt had struck his carotid artery. His eyes had a certain glassiness about them. It was apparent that my little man had fallen victim to the dreaded infection that many first-timers contract—deer fever.

As Zach struggled to hold on to consciousness, one of the does did something that made me wonder if she was dealing with some kind of death wish. She decided to come on a dead walk straight to the stand. At seven yards she turned broadside. Looking at Zach, I whispered, "This is the one!"

Seeing that his hands were weakened by the fever, I reached over and pulled the hammer back on LuLu for him. "Whenever you're ready, son, squeeze the trig…" Before I finished the last word of my command, the shooting house reverberated with a deafening BOOOOOOM! With the blast, I saw a cloud of dust instantly appear between the doe's legs. The slug had missed the doe and killed the earth.

Unbelievably, the would-have-been trophy and the other does in the field stood motionless, unsure of the cause of the explosion or that one of them had almost bit the dust. In response to her motionlessness, I carefully pulled LuLu back through the window and reloaded her.

With the doe still standing like a statue below us, I told Zach, "Try it again, dude. Put the sight on her front shoulder and squeeze one off."

This time Zach managed to take his time aiming. However, he was so overwhelmed by the effects of the fever that the end of his gun barrel looked like the checkered flag waving at Talladega Superspeedway. Now the pounding in his chest sounded like a whole tribe of little hunters was beating their drums behind his rib cage. Bless his heart! The little guy who had been rock-solid at the shooting range was shaken nearly beyond recovery in the real world where man and beast meet face-to-face.

BOOOOM! LuLu screamed again.

Once more, at a mere seven yards, the unharmed doe looked around, apparently bewildered and probably wondering, "What's with all the thunder and no clouds and rain?"

I wondered how frightened she'd be if she'd only known just how close she came to becoming freezer filler for our family.

Feeling compassion for both the deer and Zach, I resolved to call it a day. Much to Zach's surprise, I stuck my head out the window, looked the doe squarely in her big black eyes, and said, "Girl, this is your lucky day. It would be best if you vacated the premises. I'm not sure my partner up here can emotionally handle missing three times."

As I pulled my head back into the shooting house, my little man still had a blank stare on his face as he tried to take in all that had happened. He looked like he'd just had an encounter with the Bogeyman he was sure lived under his bed.

As we made our way back home, the beating of the tribal drums within Zach's ribs began to fade. His color came back, and he began to return to normal. He started talking about the experience, reliving every moment. Though his deer tag was yet to be punched, he knew, as I did, that he was now a *real* hunter with a very real gun and a very real memory to hold on to for the rest of his life.

The Lesson

"There is a time for everything, and a season for every activity under the heavens." Never did King Solomon's words ring more true as they did that evening after Zach's first official hunt. An uninitiated person might look at this story and say the season ended in total disappointment. However, that wasn't at all the case. Looking back, the season taught Zach and me some incredibly important and useful life lessons.

With his errant shots, Zach learned to not be surprised by the fact that even with our best preparation things do not always go as we plan. He also learned to try again when the situation didn't go as he'd hoped. Disappointments like missing a doe twice might shake the confidence for a while, but it can't stop a fellow from working harder at being ready for the next opportunity. And that's exactly what happened.

Zach kept hunting, and he did get his first deer. I'm thoroughly delighted to report that not only did I experience his success while sitting at his side, I was there with a video camera in hand. What an experience! The funny thing is, Zach was far more calm than I was on that hunt. Time had taught him well. Three years later, Zach took his very first buck—a great 8-point by anyone's standard. Perseverance does pay off.

Watching Zach's determination to find success in the deer woods reminded me of the extreme value of keeping a "stick to it" attitude, not just in the woods but in all the rest of life. My son will tell you that the

lessons he gleaned on the deer stand in that first season, and in all that followed, served to make him a better student, a more likeable friend, and a
more dependable teammate in sports.

The "I'm not gonna give up" attitude has served both of us in the
most important trophy pursuit of all time—being better followers of Jesus
Christ. What a joy to have learned such valuable lessons together while
deer hunting!

13

"B" Roll

by Dan Field

The level of interest I have in hunting is best described by a line in a camouflage clothing commercial I heard years ago: "It's not just a passion; it's an obsession!" How true for me. Then, as if hunting itself weren't enough to occupy my brain, several years ago I discovered another interest that grabbed my attention and held on like a boa constrictor. I became a huge fan of filming hunts.

While hunting can eat up a lot of time due to the necessary practicing, planning, and then sitting for hours in a stand, adding the element of filming puts time consumption in a whole new category. It requires being in the woods long before sunrise to set up video equipment and rehearse possible shot sequences. In addition, filming demands patiently enduring long waits to capture what can turn out to be mere seconds of action. And then there's the tear down, hauling the equipment back to the vehicle, loading it, and then making the trip back home after the hunt. Even then the job isn't finished. There's still the task of editing the film. Needless to say, being a hunter and videographer has the potential to devour all the ticks of a clock.

In reality, these two interests are, in and of themselves, well and good. That is, they would be if they were all I did. However, I have another interest that is of far greater value to me. I'm also a dad...a dad who desperately loves his children and understands how incredibly important it is to spend time with them. Striking a balance between being a father, a hunter, and videographer would be a huge challenge for me except for one wonderful fact. My kids not only took to hunting like a bear to a picnic table, they also love filming a hunt as much as I do! (And, for those who are wondering, I am married, and no, I haven't forgotten my dear wife. Thankfully, she is very agreeable to the time I spend with my kids in the outdoors. She also believes in our purpose for filming hunts, which is to inspire and encourage other hunters to see the value of stronger relationships with family and with God, our great Creator.)

While it would seem that the combination of hunting and filming and all it requires to be done successfully might result in too much distraction and threaten the creation of the strong bond my sons and I need to have, I'm happy to report that quite the opposite happened. Our teamwork with guns, bows, and cameras has yielded some of the best times any father could have with his children and will undoubtedly result in even more great memories.

For example, my eldest son, Kelin, quickly advanced through the young years and the "restless kid syndrome" to become a very experienced hunter and fellow videographer. At the time of this writing, he is attending college and is an aspiring film student. My satisfaction for being the one to have introduced Kelin to the outdoors as well as helping him discover a skill he can enjoy for the rest of his life knows no bounds. Sometimes when I'm hunting alone and reflecting on the years we had together behind the bowstring and the red button on the camera, I recall specific moments and the benefits they yielded. The joy I feel is overwhelming. One of those times happened when Kelin was an impressionable 14 year old.

Assuming the role as cameraman (and for a youngster he was quite skilled and had plenty of practice at it), Kelin was to capture me on this particular hunt. As he pressed his eye to the viewfinder to get some light settings, he pointed the lens at me and referred to me as "the talent." This was a term we'd picked up somewhere along the way and used to refer to the person being filmed. I didn't mind the reference except for the fact that Kelin always wore a mischievous grin when he said it. I knew very well I'd earned that grin because of those times when I'd totally blown a shot at an animal and/or rendered film footage useless…except for blooper outtakes.

There have been more times than I care to admit that I've made deer tremble at coming within "fling distance" of an arrow from my compound bow. The proof of their "fear" was heard in the snorts they uttered as they ran off after my poorly delivered arrow slammed noisily into a nearby sapling or hit the ground. After a bad shot, Kelin always had to work hard to keep his laughter quiet as I said things like, "That sapling needed to be culled from the tree herd" or "Dude, trees sure do grow fast around here."

Regardless of any lack of abilities that I had, on this particular morning "the talent" and his son had finally made it past "deer thirty," and we were quietly engaged in the visual search for some critters to wander into the range of my bow and his camera. As we sat in the stillness, I thought of other things than the hunt. I didn't stop looking for deer, of course, but my mind started looking at the trail that had led my eldest son and me to where we were at that moment.

We were not a father and son divided by the challenges of the teen years—by differences in music tastes, by fights over questionable friends, or by the battles dads and sons can have over the misuse or overuse of technology. Instead, we were sitting within a couple of feet of each other, focused on the exact same thing, and loving every minute of it. We were hoping this season of life would never come to an end. The feelings of gratitude I felt for the relationship we'd developed warmed me like welcome sunshine on a frigid morning. I couldn't help but whisper a prayer to my Father in heaven for helping me not make the mistake of abandoning my role as dad in order to spend more time hunting. Moments of thanksgiving to my Maker like this have happened many times since that day.

Not much was happening in the surrounding woods except for a browsing squirrel or two that came by and were startled by our presence. After another half hour passed, I thought about an adventure Kelin and I had experienced out West. I finally broke the silence using my best hunting show talent voice. "Son, I was just thinking about our recent trip to Montana. Two Indiana boys on an elk and mule deer hunt. Does it get any better than that?"

"It was awesome, Dad. Just awesome!" Kelin's eyes lit up as he remembered the trip.

"It was indeed. Do you know how long I dreamed of going to the Big Sky country on a hunt? You're probably not aware of how many times I saved nearly all the money required to make it happen, only to have to spend it on something the family needed. I knew I was doing the right thing to let the hunt go at the time, but it wasn't easy, to say the least."

"What would you do when that happened, Dad?"

I could hear in Kelin's tone that he felt my pain. Only a true hunter would feel it. "I did the only thing I could do. I took care of the crisis and started saving again. There wasn't a line for the expense of a Western hunt in the family budget, so when things like an $800 septic tank repair interfered with my plans, I had to do what was necessary. I certainly enjoyed the freedom to flush without a smelly backwash in the house, but giving up the thrill of a first kill on a Montana mountain for the convenience of pressing that little silver lever was tough to do."

Kelin smiled at my statement and revealed some regret that the camera wasn't recording when I offered such an eloquent description of my deepest feelings. Then it dawned on me that I'd unexpectedly entered into a teachable moment with my teenaged son. I realized I'd just taught him one of the most important lessons a dad can pass on to a son who would someday be a family man himself. I'd relayed a real-life example of what it means to put the family first and shown that it can sometimes demand the sacrifice of a personal dream.

I knew my son's demeanor well enough that I could read his reaction to my words. I could tell by his pensive expression that he'd input the data and pushed the save button on his mental computer. I could almost see him mentally projecting himself into time and bracing for the challenge of someday having to make the same kind of choices as a responsible husband and father. Even at his young age I believe he could feel the impact of what we'd talked about. I was beyond joyous that it seemed he'd gotten the message. I felt confident that I'd just planted a seed of genuine maturity in him. Once again I silently thanked God for the opportunity to do so. I also thanked Him for the chance to teach such a life-altering lesson to my son while sitting together in a deer stand.

In closing, there is something that every cameraman does who films "the talent" after a successful shot is made. He points the eye of the camera at the hunter and waits for his or her verbal reaction to what just happened. In the filming industry, this type of footage is called "B-roll." That morning we didn't see a deer, so there was no kill on film. Consequently, there was no afterglow B-roll to be captured. However, if Kelin had turned the camera on me and asked for my reaction to the verbal exchange we'd just had about real life and the value of personal sacrifice, I would have looked into the lens and said with all sincerity to every dad watching, "Whatever you do, make sure you include your kids in your obsession...er...your passion for the hunt. You don't want to miss one opportunity like I just had with my son. I promise you'll see your time together as real trophies, the kind you hang on your wall of memories."

Combining my roles as father, hunter, and videographer has been incredibly rewarding. Eventually, a company was formed with two of my hunting friends, Steve Rotramel and Dave McGill. ProVision Productions' mission is to build stronger relationships between fathers and children and lead hunters to a greater appreciation of our marvelous Creator. Our first national release, *Outdoor Journey*, yielded substantial success and became the launchpad for other films we've done. I feel extremely blessed to have been able to turn my passion into a mission. Check out our website: www .ProVisionProductions.net.

14

My Trophies

by Alice Click

The first morning of deer season in West Virginia for my husband, Karl, and our son, Jason, is more than just a chance to experience the thrill of filling their tags with big bucks. It is, for both of them, the moment when they can finally sit down, stop moving, and rest after many weeks of intense preparation for the first light of opening day.

Through the years I've enjoyed watching them react to the "hunting juices" that start to flow as the autumn-time progresses toward our Mountaineer State's rifle season. Their demeanor changes from a ho-hum, everyday approach to life to a fidgety restlessness. It's an anxiety that can be calmed only by feverishly working as a team toward the goal of being ready for the kickoff of another year of wild game chasing. It's a sight to see their eyes shine with expectation while they engage in a flurry of preparation that includes:

- Scouting the 125 acres of our farm for scrapes, rubs, well-used trails, and other signs that the resident deer are leaving behind. Because the deer traffic patterns don't change a lot from year to year, the "honey holes" are the first locations to be surveyed. Then they proceed to the rest of our acreage for a thorough look at the telltale evidence that the new season will provide some action.

- Making sure the homemade, elevated shooting shacks are safe by replacing old ladder rungs, testing the weight-bearing capability of the plywood floors, tearing out dry-rotted carpets and laying new if needed, replacing worn swivel chair seats and seatbacks, oiling the swivel posts for quietness of turning, checking the roofs for leaks and fixing as needed, greasing the sliding windows to avoid unwanted squeaks, and cutting away branches that might block the view and hinder rifle shots.

- Servicing the portable heater that son will take to Dad's stand the day before season opens and making sure it provides the warmth necessary for the "old man's skin" to successfully battle the frigid West Virginia, predawn winter air.

- Checking the homemade wooden treestands for safe usage and fixing any problems that are discovered, such as a rotted climbing step or a screw that has been forced out by the growth of the tree trunk. Also, looking over the pull-up strings that hoist their guns up to the platform and replacing them if they appear the least bit frayed.

- Going to the shooting range on the backside of the farm with their rifles and sighting them in…again…for the sake of feeling confident *when* (they hope), not *if*, the "moment of truth" walks into range.

- Cleaning the rifles thoroughly, and then removing as much of the pungent odor of gun oil as possible from each weapon so the local, wily whitetail noses won't pick up the scent and run to the neighboring farms.

- Testing the thermos jugs to ensure that after that first hour of opening day passes and the low temperatures make their bodies cry out for the warming taste of fresh coffee, the container will not disappoint them with a cup of cooled brew.

- Washing their camo clothing in scent-free soap, air-drying them outside on the clothesline, and then marinating every garment in a bag of dry leaves to help remove the deer-spooking, unnatural scent of laundry soap.

- Checking their boots to make sure they're in good shape—and replacing if needed.

- Buying hunting licenses and tags.

- Sharpening their knives and packing elbow-length, latex gloves for field dressing.

- Packing and repacking the bags they'll take to the stands.

- Putting new sparkplugs in the 4-wheeler.

- Removing fallen trees from the 4-wheeler trails.

I could go on and on with the details they cover each year. Even when they think they've got it all done, there is always something they've overlooked. But of all the jobs that father and son do, I know the hardest is still ahead of them when it comes to preparing for the first morning hunt of the season. I've seen them struggle with it many times through the years past. The toughest of the tasks for each of them is to go to sleep the night before opening day.

When the alarm clock rouses them (and me) at the painful hour of four o'clock, they seem to catapult out of their beds. Within minutes their zeal for what they're about to do propels them to the back door. As they gather there for the excited exit, they look to me for the traditional disbursing of the plastic grocery bags filled with biscuits, jam, ham, Snickers bars, and thermoses of coffee. Also included in the feast is a large baggie filled with peanuts-in-the-shell that were purchased from the local feed store. I gladly hand the bags to my two hunters, and they grab them like sacks of candy and offer quick-but-sincere thanks. Within 29 minutes or so from the time the alarm sounds to the closing of the door, the house that was abuzz with frantic dressing and boot lacing suddenly turns strangely quiet. I'm left to imagine what the morning will be like for my men.

In my mind's eye I see them bouncing simultaneously on the 4-wheeler as they descend the trail that takes them into the deep hollow behind our house. I see my husband gripping the handlebars and gritting his teeth to combat the icy air that is cutting at his face. I see Jason tucking his head in behind his dad's head to let the chilly, knife-edge wind bypass his face, which is smiling with anticipation despite the cold.

I imagine them parking the 4-wheeler and, just before splitting up and walking to their chosen stands, see them checking to make sure their radios are on the same frequency and the batteries are strong. Then I can see them patting each other on their backs and wishing each other the chance to pull the trigger. I can almost hear them saying the same words to one another that they've said through seasons past: "Call me if you connect, and I'll be there as quickly as I can."

Just before I drift back to sleep in my warm bed, I can almost see my husband and son quietly climbing into their shooting shacks and, at last, feeling the joy of sitting down in their freshly oiled, quiet, swivel seats and sighing deeply with contentment. I imagine them sitting there, resting in the predawn darkness, feeling satisfied that they did all they could do to be prepared for the opportunity that might come with daylight.

And then the sweetest of all thoughts crosses my mind. I imagine each of them hoping for a sighting of a wall-hanger for themselves, but knowing that in their hearts they love each other enough that they hope it happens for the other person more. This thought brings some mighty peace to my soul.

There have been some changes through the years in terms of their hunting. For example, a new and bigger 4-wheeler replaced the old, worn-out workhorse. There has been an upgrade in rifle calibers, and I've noticed a fancy, new pop-up ground blind has been added to the gear they use. But there has been one change that excites me more than anything else. There are four new hunters who get my plastic grocery bags full of deer stand snacks. Jason married a young lady named Linda who is as avid about hunting as he is. The two of them then added three other little hunters to our family: Anthony, Alexa, and Jaden. It's pure pleasure to see my grandkids following in the "hoof tracks" of their parents and granddad.

What do I get out of all the added chaos that happens now on opening morning of deer season? I get the joy of seeing how deer hunting continues to be one of the major ways that the bond between all of us is strengthened year after year. The smiles of a father and son, as well as the smiles on my daughter-in-law and grandkids' faces as they enjoy being with each other, are the trophies that hang on the wall of my heart.

15

A Big, Ol' "Atta Dad!"

by Steve Chapman

Most of us who are sons will agree there's hardly anything as sweet sounding as an "atta boy" from the lips of our fathers. Whether it comes after a base hit at the Little League diamond, or a job well done on the mower, or an improved grade in math class, it's always nice to hear a father's pride put into words. But have we ever thought about how our dads would feel if we turned the picture around and gave them a good, healthy dose of "son" pride? The following story is based on a dad named Phil and his 19-year-old son, Jamey.

Jamey's walkie-talkie buzzed in his pocket, and as he dug to retrieve it he checked the field carefully to make sure the buck he was hoping to see hadn't stepped into the open. He pushed the talk button and responded to the call. "Dad, what's going on where you are? See something?"

Jamey had the volume turned down low so the noise wouldn't spook anything in the area. He quickly put the radio close to his ear after he spoke. He smiled as his dad's voice delivered some great news.

"I just arrowed a monster over here, son. He's at least a 12, maybe bigger. I didn't take the time to count. He came in fast, and I only had a few seconds to get to full draw and pull the release trigger. All I know is he's the best deer I've ever shot with a bow. I'm shaking all over. And the best news is that he's down within sight of my stand."

Jamey heard the thrill in his father's voice and pushed the talk button to congratulate him. "Way to go, Pops! You get a big, ol' 'atta Dad' today! While you recover, I'll call Mom on the cell and tell her that her Mr. Phil just added a taxidermy job to his Christmas list."

Phil smiled at his son's response to the news about the buck. "Thanks, Jamey. I'm gonna wait about 20 minutes and then dismount. I'll start the cleaning process while you keep hunting. I'll call you when I'm done, and you can come help me drag this brute to the truck. It'll probably be about an hour from now."

"Are you kidding, Dad? I'm already packing up and just about ready to head to the ground to come to you. I can't wait an hour to see the prize you're taking home today! I'll see you in a few."

As Jamey topped the hill and saw his dad leaning over the huge body of a buck, his eyes widened. When he got to his dad, he circled him and the deer and slapped his hip in amazement. "Whoa, Pops! That thing is huge. One, two… four…five…ten…fourteen…fifteen points?"

Phil grinned big. "Yep! Fifteen points for scoring. One for every year I've been hunting with a bow. How about them beans, my boy?"

Jamey threw his arm around his dad's shoulder. "Give me a Pope & Young hug, man! This is an awesome buck! I can't wait to tell my friends about this. We gotta get some pictures. This is gonna be big news in these parts, and I'm the son of the one who flung the arrow at this trophy. You da man, Pops!"

With every sentence Jamey delivered, Phil's grin grew bigger. He couldn't remember ever being so gloated over by his son. He'd given Jamey plenty of "atta boys" while he was growing up, but they'd never been returned—until now. Phil enjoyed the accolades.

"Dad, I'm proud of you for maintaining enough calm to get a shot off at this buck."

Any other time Phil would have said, "Young man, stop talking and sharpen your knife. I can use your help." But this time he didn't want to stop his boy.

"It had to take some steady nerves to even get the string back, much less remember where to put the sight pin. I'm not sure I could've done it. I'm impressed, Pops! I'm totally impressed."

I believe that deep inside those of us who have children is an unspoken hope that we will hear something similar to what Jamey told his dad that day. No doubt a father like Phil would carry his son's words in his heart like a priceless pearl and wouldn't take a farm in Montana for them. But what dad wouldn't feel the same way?

As I listened to Phil and Jamey's story unfold, I thought of the first time I offered my dad some praise. It didn't involve a deer hunt, but I remember the look of satisfaction on his face when it happened. That moment was just as huge to him as if he'd taken a 15-pointer.

My dad was a self-taught preacher, and he pastored a congregation of believers in Christ in the town of Point Pleasant, West Virginia. I watched him head to the basement of our house many times to spend hours preparing sermons to deliver to the people. My mother, sister, and I would always be in the pews when he stood at the pulpit to encourage the saints as well as "call the sinners home." The meeting would end, and our family would all go back to our house, usually without saying much about the service or the sermon, except a comment or two from Mom.

Dad didn't seem to require compliments from the attendees or his family to keep delivering the truth. Sunday after Sunday he was faithful to God's call to preach. And service after service we would listen and go home. It was rather routine to me, and sometimes a bit on the mundane side of the fun spectrum. That is until one Sunday when I really listened to what Dad was saying in his message to his congregation.

As he preached that morning, I was so grateful for something he'd said that I suddenly got an odd thought. *Have I ever thanked Dad? No, I've never thanked him for a single sermon he's preached in my 17 years of being his kid.* I decided at that moment to compliment him on the well-prepared and inspiring message he was delivering that morning.

When the service was over and we got home, I got out of our car and walked beside him up the sidewalk. I put my arm around his shoulder and simply said, "Great sermon, Dad. I enjoyed every word."

I'll never forget how he looked at me in that instant. His eyes shone and lit up the smile that filled his face. He almost acted like a teenager when he bypassed the first two concrete steps of our front porch and jumped straight to the landing in a single bound. It was easy to see that he felt lighter on his feet from the compliment. He was even a little more talkative at the lunch table than he normally was after an emotionally draining Sunday-morning service.

I was convinced that day that my simple-but-sincere "atta Dad" had pleased my father in an unusually special way. And it felt really good on my part to be such a source of encouragement. After all, he'd been doing the same for me all along. I determined to offer more "atta Dads" in the future, and I followed through.

A few years ago I documented my appreciation for his life via a song lyric. This is the highest compliment I can pay to the greatest preacher I've ever known and the best sermon ever preached. I hope you enjoy it.

Daddy's Best Sermon

Daddy was good at preaching the Word,
About the best I've ever heard.
He could help a sinner know he was lost,
Then lead him home by the way of the Cross.

He could help a saint want to hold on tighter,
Say the right thing to make a burden feel lighter.
But of all the sermons Daddy ever preached,
The one that meant the most to me…

Was the way he loved me and my sister,
And how he held our mama's hand, and the tender way he kissed her.
Who he was on Sunday afternoon,
With just us in the living room.
Yeah, Daddy's best sermon, he preached at home.

I remember growing-up sitting in the pews,
While Daddy brought the Good News.
I could almost see the angels smile,
When sinners cried and walked down the aisle.

People came to hear him from all around,
I never knew him to let them down.
'Cause he was good at breaking the bread,
But my soul had a hunger that he always fed.

It was the way he loved me and my sister,
And how he held our mama's hand, and the tender way he kissed her.
Who he was on Sunday afternoon,
With just us in the living room.
Daddy's best sermon, he preached at home.[1]

As a son who encouraged his dad and enjoyed the benefits, I can confidently say that if you'll take the next opportunity that arises to give your dad some heartfelt praise for something he's done or does, you too will enjoy what can happen. You might get to see your dad smile in a way you've never seen before. And his steps might get a little lighter too. And someday the bread you cast on the waters of his heart could very well come back to you.

16

The Empty Treestand

by Brad Herndon

It was the middle of the night and was bitterly cold. My dad, Paul, was in the army, and my mom, Doris, lived with my grandmother, Freda (Nanny) Leffler, in a house high on a hill near southern Indiana's Jackson County Forestry. Like all unborn babies, the time had come for me to see my first light in this world. Mom and Nanny piled in the car that had always started easily. Alarmingly, the battery was too weak to turn the engine over. Quickly they pushed the car off the hill, and despite popping the clutch numerous times, "Old Reliable" never fired—not even one time. It was only after they got to the bottom of the hill that they discovered they'd never turned the ignition key.

They walked back up the hill to get the "backup" car. Soon they were at the bottom of the hill once more, again without a running vehicle. It was only by awakening a nearby neighbor who had a newer car that did start that Mom was able to get to the hospital so I could be delivered in normal fashion. The day was February 16. Obviously, I got an interesting start in life. I appreciate my mom and grandmother passing their recollections of my birth on to me so I also have them in my memory bank.

One of my earliest memories is about a time when I was around six years old. We lived in the country, and one evening as darkness had just enveloped the forest, I saw a storm coming in. Storms fascinated me even then, so I sat down on our porch. As I watched the lightning in the approaching clouds, a feeling came over me that I've never forgotten. As

I watched the majesty of the storm, I sensed that someone was out there. Even more amazingly, I felt that "someone" loved me. I didn't realize it at the time, but I would later learn the "someone" was God preparing me for a day when I would need to know He would be present even in the storms of life.

My family moved around some before my dad got out of the army. By the time I entered sixth grade, we'd settled in Starve Hollow, a peaceful valley in the hills near where I was born. I loved living there because I could hunt rabbits, quail, and squirrels. Fishing was nearby, and so were abundant mushrooms, nuts, and berries to pick and eat. Birds, insects, reptiles, and other fascinating creatures made daily life interesting.

My mom and grandmother were experts about nature, and they could answer most of the many questions I had regarding what I saw or found while roaming the countryside. My dad stayed in the city all week where he worked, but on the weekends he taught me gun safety and gave me tips about hunting strategies.

Except for my grandmother, our family didn't attend church. My dad didn't care for it, and though my mom would love to have attended, she wasn't able to because she didn't drive. Despite this upbringing, when I was in the outdoors during my teenage years I still felt the presence of the "one in the mighty clouds" I'd encountered at the age of six.

During my formative years I was blessed to have a mother who would listen to my every outdoor adventure with interest and patience, paying attention to every detail since she too loved to roam the hills and hollers. Time passed, and finally in 1961 the teachers—probably with a sigh of relief—allowed me to graduate and enter the real world.

Cruising Pays Off

As a teenager, I was a "cruiser." Cruising, or "scooping the loop" as many of us called it back then, was when a young man or young woman went to town on Friday and Saturday nights and drove up and down main street (main drag) looking for cute chicks or handsome guys. In my day, cruising was rather harmless. In fact, at times the practice turned out rather well. One time when I was cruising in Seymour, Indiana, I met a cute little gal named Carol Casey. This meeting eventually led to our marriage! After a while we purchased a small log home and three acres. Carol took to the outdoors like a duck takes to water.

On August 15, approximately 12 months after our marriage, Carol gave birth to our first child, a son we named Joseph Bradley. We were very excited about his birth, of course, but I was especially excited that his birth fell on the first day of squirrel season, my favorite type of hunting. Looking into the future, I could hardly wait to tell him about the unforgettable adventures I'd experienced during my journey as a hunter. I got excited as I envisioned both of us making our own memories while squirrel, rabbit, and quail hunting. I could also see him meandering the hills with Carol and me as we shared all we knew about nature with him. Yes, life was good. And with the arrival of a little hunting buddy, I was sure it was going to get even better.

Life Isn't Always Easy

Because Carol was sick when she gave birth to Joseph Bradley, we went to my mom and dad's home so Mom could help with the baby. On his eighth day of life here on earth, Carol and mom noticed Joseph was sick… and getting sicker. Carol and I rushed him to the nearby Seymour hospital, and then from there he went by ambulance to Children's Hospital in Louisville, Kentucky.

We waited in the emergency room, hoping our baby was going to be all right. Finally a doctor came into the waiting room. He had a terribly distressed look on his face, and after some hesitation he finally said four of the most dreadful words any parent could ever hear: "Your baby is dead."

Carol and I were crushed by the death of our son. It was especially hard on my wife since she'd carried the baby in her womb for so long. Our recovery from Joseph Bradley's death was difficult, to say the least. Carol was a Christian, and although I wasn't then, I would often go back to that distant childhood moment when I'd encountered God in the storm clouds. I eventually realized that He is always in control, and that He is also here when the storm clouds of life hit hardest.

In my search for answers about our great loss, I started reading the Bible. I read about a man in the Old Testament named David who did a vile thing. A powerful king, this man took another man's wife, Bathsheba, and committed adultery with her. Then, to hide his sin, David arranged to have her husband Uriah killed in battle.

Bathsheba became pregnant from the adulterous relationship, and a baby boy was born. Shortly thereafter, God confronted David by having the prophet Nathan relate a simple parable to convict the king of his sins.

David immediately admitted his iniquity, repented, and asked for God's forgiveness. And God did forgive David of his many sins. But there were consequences for David. God struck the baby with an illness. David prayed for the baby to live, wore sackcloth, and wouldn't eat or take care of himself. Sadly, the baby died. Second Samuel 12:19-23 describes what happened after the death of the child:

> When David saw that his servants were whispering together, David perceived that the child was dead; so David said to his servants, "Is the child dead?" And they said, "He is dead." So David arose from the ground, washed, anointed himself, and changed his clothes; and he came into the house of the LORD and worshiped. Then he came to his own house, and when he requested, they set food before him and he ate.
>
> Then his servants said to him, "What is this thing that you have done? While the child was alive, you fasted and wept; but when the child died, you arose and ate food." He said, "While the child was still alive, I fasted and wept; for I said, 'Who knows, the LORD may be gracious to me, that the child may live.' But now he has died; why should I fast? Can I bring him back again? I will go to him, but he will not return to me."

David knew his baby could never return to him, but he knew with God's mercy he could go to his baby! This Scripture forever changed my life! I knew there was a God, and I knew the only way Carol and I could be united with our baby once again was to join him in heaven. The problem was, unlike Carol, I hadn't yet figured out how to get there.

I Will Go to Him

After much prayer, soul searching, and study of the Bible, God convicted me of my numerous sins. I was convinced Jesus Christ was the way, the truth, and the life, and no one could get to God the Father, and heaven, except through Him (John 14:6). I repented of my sins, asked for forgiveness, and accepted Jesus Christ into my life as my personal Savior.

Since becoming a Christian, my days have become full of hope, despite life's occasional setbacks. Three years after Joseph Bradley's birth and death, Carol and I had a daughter we named JoLinda. She has a sweet, loving, sharing personality and was a joy to raise. She grew up spending incredible amounts of time with us amid nature. She fished. She gathered berries, nuts, mushrooms, ginseng, asparagus, and many other examples of nature's bounty with us. She canoed and hiked hundreds of miles. Interestingly, she wasn't interested in hunting during those years.

Now, years later, one of JoLinda's daughters, Jessica, "the Rascal Girl," is a deer and turkey hunter. Even JoLinda's husband, Curt, who is originally from Chicago, is harvesting whitetails. And recently JoLinda told us she's ready to buy a hunting license for the first time!

No Empty Treestands in Heaven

When I was a youngster and telling my hunting stories to Mom, I had no idea I would become an outdoor writer specializing in deer hunting stories or a photographer specializing in deer hunting images. Nor did I imagine my wife would spend as much time hunting deer and other varieties of game as I did. It's been a blessed time for us. But in our minds throughout the years, there's always been an empty treestand in our deer hunting area. It's the one Joseph Bradley would have been sitting in.

Perhaps there is an empty treestand where your family hunts deer too. It could be because you too have lost a son or a daughter. Or maybe it's a result of the death of a parent, grandparent, brother, sister, uncle, aunt, cousin, or friend. I believe God has brought me to this place in life—to this story—so I can share the good news of Jesus Christ with you. I want to assure you there is great hope for your future regardless of the magnitude of your loss. Jesus told us, "In My Father's house are many mansions; if it were not so, I would have told you. I go to prepare a place for you" (NKJV).

Carol and I want to see Joseph Bradley again, just as you want to see your loved ones someday. We think our daughter, JoLinda, her husband, Curt, and their children, Hannah and Jessica, will be thrilled to meet him. We want the rest of our family to know Joseph Bradley too. We would love for you to meet him as well.

The good news is that we all can see our loved ones who have gone to heaven if we accept the sacrifice Jesus Christ made on a cross, giving His life for our many sins and thereby cleansing us from all unrighteousness. The gift has been given. Eternal life with Jesus in heaven is available if you will only accept Him as your Lord and Savior.

If you are already a Christian, I encourage you to study the Bible. God will reveal many comforting passages that will give you hope in life and joy for the future. If you're not a Christian, I pray you will read the Bible with an open mind. Let God reveal Himself to you. Remember my dad? He wasn't interested in going to church. Late in his life he changed. He died a smiling Christian and a saved man by the grace of God.

As I write this, Carol and I are closing in on the lifespan mentioned in the Bible—seventy years (Psalm 90:10). We still tremendously enjoy nature and look forward to spending considerable time outside each day. And yet we also joyfully look forward to the future when we will dwell on this earth no more. We know there will be no empty treestands in heaven.

17

An Eye for the Hunt

by Dan Swartz

It was Friday afternoon in the last week of October. My wife, Sherri, was at her work at the library, and I was home with our only child, a two-year-old daughter named Brianna. I was trying to be a good and dependable dad, but I was facing a dilemma that only a die-hard deer hunter would understand. As my lovely little girl played at my feet, I stood at the window and looked outside. It was nearing 3:00, and I knew the weather was perfect for an evening hunt—not too cold, not too hot. I watched the clock tick the minutes away and felt that familiar restlessness that comes when my heart is in the deer stand but my body can't join it because of domestic duties.

I picked up my toddler and held her so she could see outside. "See what Daddy's giving up for you, little girl? I sure would like to be out there sitting in my stand, but..." I stopped mid-sentence, and Brianna looked at me with a puzzled expression. Even a two-year-old could tell I'd been interrupted and was looking for words to say. I looked at her as I processed the idea that had just jumped into my head. "Brianna, how would you like to go hunting with Daddy?"

I knew very well that the only words my tiny daughter understood in my question was "go with Daddy." I was also sure that her immediate "yes" reply had nothing to do with a desire to hunt whitetails, but that realization didn't stop me. I was convinced I had just come upon the best idea I'd had in a long time. There were a few challenges to my plan that passed through my logical brain. *What will Sherri think when she finds out I've taken Brianna to the deer stand with me? How am I going to hunt with a wiggly toddler? What would I do if I connected with a deer and following the blood trail lasted into the dark of night?* Like I said, those challenges passed right through my head. I intentionally didn't entertain them for long because I knew if I thought about them long enough, I would conclude taking Brianna hunting wasn't a smart thing to do.

I did, however, entertain more hunter-friendly thoughts. *This might be a harebrained idea but I can pull this off. Besides, what better bonding time could I possibly have with my daughter than sitting with her in a deer blind? It's never too early to get 'em started on the trail to adventure!*

Armed with my best argument, I quickly gathered up a few of Brianna's little colorful books, some crayons, a few sheets of typing paper, a stuffed animal, a pack of graham crackers, a sippy cup filled with apple juice, and, of course, all my hunting gear. I managed to get all the necessary items packed up. With Brianna dressed in some warm clothes, she and I walked out the front door and headed to the truck.

I was a little worried that a hunting buddy might drive by and see what I was doing and stop to ask if I'd lost my mind. Worse yet, what if Sherri came home for some reason just as I was loading the truck? As I wrestled with these worries, I decided to do what any deer hunter would do. I double-timed the loading process, fired up the truck, and took off.

The walk from where I parked at the edge of the woods to the enclosed stand was mere minutes, and by 3:45 my little hunter and I were settled in. As we waited for the local deer to arrive, I was thankful that all Brianna's motions were concealed to the deer world. The only thing I had to keep reminding her to not do was tromp around on the wooden floor of the enclosure. Other than that, she seemed to be having a good time as she colored and stuffed herself with graham crackers and juice.

There I was with my little girl, sitting out in the middle of God's great outdoors. I whispered, "Does it get any better than this?" Well, yes, it does. As I was basking in the glow of the good feelings, a young spike suddenly appeared about 75 yards away. A couple of does were following behind him. I was looking for a bigger buck to bag, so I had no intention of taking a shot. However, I knew this was a perfect scene for my little one to watch.

I carefully picked her up and sat her on my lap. I slowly pointed to the trio of deer. "Brianna, can you see the three deer? Look over Daddy's finger, and you'll see them." I could feel her little body slightly jump when her eyes caught sight of the animals. I could tell she wanted to squeal with excitement, so I put my index finger to my mouth, quietly said "shh," and smiled. "How cool is that, Brianna? We have to be quiet. If those deer know we're here, they'll get nervous and run away. Let's just sit really still and watch them, okay?"

"Okay, Daddy." Her little voice seemed to tremble with joy as she responded softly.

I did everything I could to contain my own desire to shout, "This is so awesome!" The two of us quietly watched the three visitors until they disappeared deeper into the woods.

Brianna didn't know that the whole time she observed the deer I was taking note of how she acted as she watched them. It appeared to me that because she didn't take her eyes off the animals and was willingly sitting motionless and quiet, maybe…just maybe…I had a bona fide hunting partner sitting in my lap.

As it turned out, all we did that afternoon was watch deer. A few more wandered by, but nothing I wanted to shoot. Still, the hunt ended with far greater success than I ever imagined. The afternoon hunt came to a close when the sun dropped behind the west side of our state of Ohio, but a new day had dawned in my life as a dad and hunter. Brianna enjoyed her time in the woods with her daddy, and the proof of it came in the form of a question during the ride home.

"When can we go again to the box house, Daddy?"

"How about tomorrow evening, sweetheart? Is that soon enough?"

"Yeah!"

Thus began our journey together into the whitetails' woods. Twelve years and a lot of trips into the woods of the Buckeye state later, Brianna and I were headed out again. Just like many times before, we sat side-by-side and watched for incoming "freezer fare" while quietly reminiscing about past hunts. We also talked about present subjects, such as school, friends, boys, fashion, and even some spiritual matters.

Though our conversations weren't always about whitetails, we were always on the lookout for a big rack. We'd seen a couple of nice bucks earlier that year, and the signs in nature said the rut was just around the corner. We were especially hoping to see a buck I'd nicknamed "Noodles." He was a mainframe 12-point with four additional stickers protruding out in random directions. He was the type of buck most hunters refer to as a "wall hanger." On one earlier hunt, he'd been close enough that we could see him chewing on acorns, but he was just outside of what we considered our arrow range.

As we sat in the stand, I reminded Brianna that this particular hunt had a major difference than our previous outings. This time she'd been in full control. She'd been in charge of laying out the buck lure, checking the wind direction, and ensuring an arrow was set in the cocked crossbow. I commended her for effectively covering all the details and told her how impressed I was. We talked about how it couldn't have been a more perfect day. The wind was so calm we could almost hear a falling leaf hit the forest floor.

We were talking about what would happen if ol' Noodles showed up when Brianna stopped and put her hand up to stop the conversation. "Hear that?" she whispered.

I did hear it and smiled at the sight of how big my daughter's eyes had widened. The leaves nearby were crackling under the steps of something moving underneath our stand. Crunch…crunch. We could tell it wasn't a fast-footed squirrel or a scratching turkey. The sound was heavier and different.

"That's gotta be a deer!" Brianna whispered. Every muscle in our bodies tightened with excitement.

Elation turned to frustration when I looked through the brush and initially identified the critter as an unusually large coyote. I grabbed my binoculars to get a closer look at the predator, and then I realized it was a case of mistaken identity. Sure enough, Brianna was right. It was not only a deer—it was a big male. It wasn't Noodles, but it had to be his brother! A very nice nine-point buck was on the move with his head lowered as he browsed on the acorns that had dropped to the ground. The brute was way too nice to pass up!

I coached Brianna to get ready for the shot. Slowly the buck walked within range…25 yards…20 yards. "Wait, girl, wait." Then 15 yards. "Wait…"

It's strange how time slows down in moments like we were experiencing.

Lots of thoughts were flashing through the mind. "Hallelujah! She's waiting…and she's using her aiming eye." Though the words were few in number, they reflected a ton of memories. I thought of how often I'd attempted to teach Brianna that patience is a virtue, and how many times I'd longed for her to grow up with that valuable skill. I wanted her to understand the value of waiting because I knew it would serve her well in so many areas of life. I'd used hunting as a classroom for teaching her why and how to wait.

I was thankful that Brianna and I were here together, looking for deer, and that she would be able to take advantage of the opportunity to bag a deer if it came. Just the year before, our sweet daughter had gone through an ordeal that seriously tested her patience and ability to wait that she'd learned in the woods.

A Severe Testing

Brianna was in school, and class had just gotten underway. She was looking at the white board and taking notes as the teacher lectured. Suddenly Brianna noticed that the sight in her right eye was a little blurry. Within a few minutes, all sight in that eye was lost. Thinking it was momentary and that it would come back quickly, she continued to pay attention and try to take notes.

But when it didn't improve, she finally let her teacher know. The school sent her home, and Sherri and I took her right away to our family eye doctor. Although he found nothing wrong, he strongly urged us to schedule an appointment with a specialist as soon as possible. Within a few days, Sherri took Brianna to a specialty eye center about 20 minutes from our home. After several in-depth eye exams and an MRI, the results were still inconclusive. After yet one more referral to a neuro-ophthalmologist 65 miles away, he too could find nothing that would cause loss of vision. This unknown diagnosis was perplexing to my wife and me, and Brianna became deeply discouraged as she worried that she would never have normal vision again.

That year hunting season arrived without our usual level of excitement. Opening day came with hardly a mention of adventures in the woods. Instead, the family's focus was on Brianna's ailing eye. Our 10-year-old son, Brandon, had also grown to like hunting. This year only the two of us went to the stand, but Brianna's absence was like a cloud hanging over each trip. Brandon and I agreed that a big piece of the family hunting picture was missing. We tried to encourage her to go with us, but not being able to actually hunt was too difficult for her. The heartaches were gut wrenching all the way around.

A lot of family and friends were praying for Brianna's healing and for guidance on what we should do next. God raised up some wonderful friends to help our daughter through this difficult trial of partial blindness. Like brave nurses on a battlefield, the girls stepped in and assisted her with everyday tasks, such as getting safely from building to building and making sure she had all the notes she needed for studying.

I gradually realized God was using the situation to change Brianna and her closest friends. Sherri and I desperately wanted our daughter's sight to be fully restored, but with all the positive things being birthed out of such a negative thing, we decided to add to our prayers for healing that God would complete a work in our daughter that would help mature her. We asked for peace of mind and an extra measure of patience as He worked all things for the good of those who love Him (Romans 8:28). We took courage from the fact that Brianna seemed to be willing to wait on God's timing for her healing. We realized that we too needed to do the same.

As we waited that fall to see if Brianna would regain her sight in the affected eye, I was able to share some special time with her outside of hunting. I helped with homework and gladly drove her to school events, such as football games. Even though we were sharing time together, there was an unspoken fear in my heart that the lack of usefulness of her aiming eye and her subsequent absence from the woods might cause my daughter to lose interest in hunting. I dreaded the possibility because I wanted to continue to share that passion with her. I wanted her with me in the hunter's woods. While I totally enjoy hunting with my son, there is a uniqueness about hunting with my daughter that I worried would be lost.

Thankfully, by December that year Brianna began to experience some improvement in her vision. A few weeks before Christmas we took Brianna to the eye doctor for another appointment. Following more tests, it was discovered that her eye had been restored to its full ability! You can imagine the happy look on Brianna's face as the doctor announced the good news. My daughter looked at me with the familiar expression I'd been waiting for months to see again. I could detect it in the twinkle of her aiming eye. Without a word being spoken, she was saying, "It's time to go hunting again, Daddy!"

There were a few weeks of deer season left in Ohio, and Brianna, Brandon, and I went, and went, and went hunting. No shots were fired; no tags were punched. But the season was a great success simply because we were hunting together again. Brandon's joy was just as huge that his sis was with us in the hut. It was a great finish to a season that had started like a wet firecracker.

Back to That Nine-point Buck…

A year had passed, and now here Brianna and I were, sitting snug in our "box house," a nine-point buck within range, and her crossbow ready. I wished with all that was in me that Brandon had been free from school activities to see what was about to happen. The heavy-bodied beast stopped, looked around for a few seconds, and then gave a guttural grunt. The sound made us shiver with excitement. I quickly glanced at Brianna to make sure she was ready.

Before I could get out the words "take the shot," she pulled the crossbow trigger and the bolt screamed toward the deer. The familiar thump that an arrow makes when it punctures the rib cage of a deer instantly reached my ears. The entire arrow disappeared into the buck's "boiler room." Just like someone had kicked all four of its powerful legs out from under him, the brute dropped to the ground, bouncing a bit under its falling weight. He'd just encountered the nail-driving accuracy of a determined, teenaged crossbow shooter. My elation was as immediate and unbridled as the look of "I did it!" that immediately lit up Brianna's face. It was like the rays of light that hit a field when a cloud moves out of the sun's way.

Brianna and I have talked many times about that nine-point moment. We've discussed how much of that particular hunt was a clinic on waiting. It wasn't just holding as still as a statue and patiently letting the buck step within the limited range of a lightweight crossbow bolt. It was much more than that. It was months of waiting for God to bring healing and hope to a situation that could have been permanently debilitating. We've agreed many times that we need to always be thankful that her eye was restored to full sight. We're also grateful that her vision, both physical and spiritual, is dedicated to the God who gave her the healing.

After the ordeal that our family went through with Brianna's near loss of her aiming eye, our favorite verse from the Bible became the well-known admonition in Psalm 46:10: "Be still, and know that I am God" (NIV). And what better place could a dad share such a life-changing bit of wisdom with his children than in a deer stand?

18

First and Only—Maybe

by Steve Chapman

If the friendship between two guys was a pie, hardly anything could sweeten it more than having a lot in common. Such is the case with me and my friend and hunting buddy Lindsey Williams. To name just a few of the things we closely share besides a deep love of chasing critters, we both are past the 50 mark in age (I'm a little further down the road of time), each of us married way up by saying our "I do's" to West Virginia girls, and we both love the Lord. In addition, our families go to the same church, we live in the country outside the city of Nashville, we both have generated grocery cash by making music, and we both thoroughly enjoy wrestling with a lyric until the "little greasy lyrical pig" is captured.

There have also been a couple of instances where it has been down-right spooky about how linked our lives are. One is funny; the other not so laughable. The first example involves septic systems.

It was a Friday afternoon when the main sewer line running from my house to the tank in the front yard broke in half. Annie and I didn't realize it had happened until someone flushed the commode a couple of times and the washing machine pumped a load of laundry water through the line. The result was a nasty-smelling backup of sewer water spilling over the rim of the commode, which was located in the lowest section of our residence.

Annie scrambled to get a mop, a bucket, and some rubber boots and gloves. I hurriedly flipped through the Yellow Pages in search of some professional help. We'd used a particular company a few times, but they'd gone out of business, so I quickly scanned the names of other companies. My eyes fell on one name that told me I could probably trust the owner. I quickly dialed the number listed for "Stinky Pinky Septic Service."

When I told the lady on the phone about our problem, she had good news for us. The crew worked on Saturdays! She promised they would be at our house first thing the next morning. And, indeed, they showed up— all five of them. Within three hours the broken line was replaced, and we were back to a good flow.

The leader of the crew told me they had another job to go to that was about 35 miles away "as the crow flies." I gladly paid them and watched the two pink trucks (of course they were pink!) pull out of the driveway. As I stood over the repair site and smiled about the fix being done so quickly, my cell phone rang. It was Lindsey.

"Hey, man, what's up?" I asked.

Lindsey sounded a little rattled. "Oh, not much, except for the fact that we have sewer problems at our house that started early this morning. Seems our mainline to our tank has busted."

I couldn't believe my ears! Lindsey couldn't either when I said, "Dude, a crew was just here and repaired the exact same problem for us. They just pulled out of my driveway. Did you call someone to fix your line?"

"Sure did! And I can't believe they could come so quickly and on a weekend."

"Who'd you call?"

"Stinky Pinky!"

I started laughing as I responded to the incredible "coincidence" that had just happened. "Man, the Stinky Pinky crew just left my house!"

"What? Are you kidding?"

I chuckled. "Nope. Those boys are headed your way as we speak. Brace yourself for one of the most efficient crews of septic experts you'll ever see. They won't be there long, but they'll get 'er done right!"

We are still amazed that our septic systems chose to give us problems at the same time and how uncanny it was that we called the exact same company. The only explanation for mutually choosing Stinky Pinky is that we both were intrigued enough by the name that we assumed we'd fit right in with the crew.

Another time our lives strangely intersected was much more significant than the sewer system event. Less than two days after we sat in a hunting blind together and took the one-and-only turkey found in that spring gobbler season, I got a call from Susan, Lindsey's wife.

"Steve, Lindsey was out chopping firewood when he got the achy left arm feeling and the sweats. I suspected what was happening, and I called 911. Right now we're in an ambulance on our way to St. Thomas Hospital. The paramedics confirmed he's had a heart attack."

I cringed at the news, told Susan we'd get our prayer chain started, and then Annie and I would take off for the hospital.

As we sat quietly in the waiting room with the Williams family, I began to think about how much Lindsey and I shared in common and a sobering thought crossed my mind. *Okay, our brotherhood can boast quite a few similarities in regard to our lives, but I think I'll let Lindsey have full rights to this heart attack thing.*

Thankfully, the bypass surgery was completed successfully. We were much relieved. With rehab and regular exercise, Lindsey returned to his normal, lively self. About two months went by, and all was well…

Until Susan got a frantic phone call from Annie.

"Steve is in Idaho at a missions conference, and he's on his way to an emergency room at this moment. He's having heart palpitations. That's all I know at the moment. Please pray!"

Who would believe that once again our lives overlapped—and in such a significant way. I'm grateful to report that the outcome of my episode didn't require going under the knife. But still…Lindsey and I think it's uncanny that within a short amount of time we both needed to go through the doors of an emergency room with the same body part problem.

In addition to all these items, Lindsey and I have one more noteworthy similarity. We both have two children—a son and a daughter. In regard to our sons, though mine is older than Lindsey's, both have an intense passion for making music and using the latest technology to produce it. As dads, Lindsey and I encourage them in their passion. As avid hunters, we think it a bit odd that the boys seem to be drawn more to music than hunting.

My son, Nathan, has gone with me through the years and tagged several nice game animals, including deer and elk. We've also chased and caught some turkey, squirrel, and rabbit. Today his life is extremely busy with his family and music work, so I fully understand that hunting is an activity that, for now, needs to simmer on the back burner of his heart. But whenever he wants to revisit the excitement of going on a hunt, I'm ready to go!

As for Lindsey, his son, Beau, had never been on a whitetail hunt or expressed an interest in hunting. The possibility that he might never develop a penchant for hunting was reinforced when Lindsey and I finally convinced Beau to go on a deer hunt with us when he was around 14.

The day was overcast, but the threat of rain didn't dampen our plans to meet at a farm in Cheatham County, Tennessee. Furthermore, the setup for Lindsey and Beau would be in a comfortable, dry, elevated shooting house that overlooked a good-sized field that deer frequented.

Once Lindsey and Beau settled in, Lindsey loaded his .270 and watched the area for deer movement. Beau broke out his Game Boy. With the device on mute, he kept his head down and his eyes on the little screen. After a half hour had passed, Beau announced that the hard bench was making his derriere hurt.

Lindsey smiled and said, "It's part of the adventure, son. The pain will keep you awake and help you stay alert as you hunt."

Beau didn't buy his dad's veiled attempt to invite him to help keep watch on the field for incoming deer. Instead, he buried his mind into the Game Boy again and continued clicking buttons with his thumbs.

Feeling battered on the rear, Beau shifted around to find some relief. Lindsey reminded him that making noise wouldn't contribute to the success of the hunt. Even though they were well concealed inside the shooting house, he explained that deer are alert and have great hearing. In turn, the request to sit still didn't contribute to Beau's affection for where he was. The needle of his "restless meter" pegged even more to the right.

Convinced that Beau wasn't going to engage in the hunt, Lindsey decided it was time to get out of the shooting house and spend the rest of the evening walking around to find the deer. As he stood and opened the door on the floor that revealed the ladder to the ground, Beau grabbed his dad's arm.

"Hey! There's a deer standing down there, Dad," he whispered while pointing at the ground directly below them. "Right there! See it?"

Lindsey leaned over and carefully peeked down at the field. Sure enough, there stood a doe that appeared to weigh about 90 pounds. Considering it to be enough to help fill his freezer, Lindsey immediately changed his plans about leaving.

That's when things started happening fast.

Beau told his dad later that when he pointed the doe out to him he thought, *Oh no! If he shoots that deer we'll be here another two hours!*

Lindsey quickly put his ear protectors on, poked his .270 out of the shooting house door, warned his son to cover his ears, pushed the safety button to the "off" position, and pulled the trigger. The mortally wounded doe took off in the direction it had probably come. As the two of them looked toward where the deer ran, another deer appeared on their left. With the legal limit being three does a day, Lindsey put the crosshairs on it and pulled the trigger again. Within a few minutes there were two heaps of fresh venison waiting to be cleaned and made ready for the trip to the processor.

Beau couldn't believe what he'd just witnessed. One minute it was totally quiet with nothing happening other than the seemingly slow passage of time. The next minute the shooting house was filled with intense emotion, the field seemed to instantly fill with deer running everywhere, and then a very loud gun blast rattled the walls. And if that wasn't enough thrilling chaos, the first shot was followed by the sound of a rifle's bolt action, a short pause for aiming, and then a second heart-thumping explosion.

Lindsey hoped the sudden wave of excitement would entice his son to consider becoming a hunter. But then he worried that the time tracking blood trails and field dressing two deer might squelch the idea. He was quite surprised when Beau willingly joined him in the challenge of finding and following the droplets of blood that led them to the pair of deer. He was even more surprised when Beau didn't get squeamish while he held the flashlight as Lindsey took his razor-sharp knife and opened up the first deer's underside like slicing a fresh watermelon. Amazingly, the sight of blood and guts didn't faze Beau.

Lindsey wondered if his teenager's undaunted reaction to the grossness of the sight and smell of deer innards was a sign of hope that he might want to come back to the field someday as a licensed hunter. As much as he wished Beau would say, "Dad, this was fun. We gotta do this again!" the words weren't heard.

Beau went home that evening with a great memory of being in the wild with his dad and the experience of some very intense and exciting moments. But he didn't acquire a zeal for hunting.

Lindsey and I have talked about how our sons aren't captivated by deer hunting like we are. We recognize that some people don't feel an innate drive to hunt. They might like making guns go bang and enjoy the challenge of putting holes as close as possible to the center mark on paper targets, but putting holes in animals that make them bleed and die is something that doesn't strongly appeal to some of them.

The fact that one kid might be passionate about hunting while another doesn't possess an interest is clearly illustrated in the biblical story of Esau and Jacob. In Genesis 25, the Bible offers a very clear distinction between the two boys. Esau is called "a skillful hunter, a man of the field," and Jacob is referred to as "a peaceful man, living in tents" (verse 27). Each man was wired to find different things appealing. Isaac, their father, made no attempt to change the core character of either one of them. He accepted them as they were.

Taking our cue from God's Word, Lindsey and I also accept our sons for who they are. God didn't make a mistake when He didn't put blaze-orange blood in their veins like He did ours. While we believe God could use the great outdoors to teach our boys a lot through the challenge of hunting, we trust Him to teach them life lessons through the things they avidly enjoy and participate in. Whether it's through a guitar, a mixing board, new music software, a bicycle, a camera, or whatever, we are confident God will use the best platform to speak into their lives.

To date, the "double doe" hunt was Beau's first-and-only experience in the deer woods. While it very well could be the single deer-hunting story he'll ever have to tell, time might change things. After all, there was a "thrill seed" planted when the action started that day. Someday it might take root and grow. Until then, Lindsey will dream of getting this call from Beau: "Hey, Dad, can we go deer hunting again?"

19

Double Whammy

by Randy Petrich

A verse of Scripture that has become very dear to me over the years is Psalm 37:4: "Delight yourself in the LORD; and He will give you the desires of your heart." I can testify that the promise God made in this verse is one He will keep. I've seen proof of it in two areas of my life.

Because I've made God my delight, He has granted me the desire that was born in my heart at a very young age—to be a professional hunting guide. He's not only blessed my guide service with plenty of success and longevity, but He has also guided me to making it an effective opportunity to share Him with those who call on me as a guide. I'm humbled by the reality that there are hunters all across the nation who have been introduced to Christ while in the incredible beauty of the Montana mountains where I live.

An even greater way God has proven to me that He'll bless those who delight themselves in Him is by giving my wife, Dena, and me three wonderful sons. I'm blessed to be their dad. I admit, though, that being a full-time hunting guide and outfitter, along with being the father of three boys who are avid hunters, has created some very interesting challenges over the years. Before any of my boys were of legal age to hunt in our home state of Montana, I assumed that because I made my living from hunting they would either love the sport or want nothing to do with it. Thankfully, all three boys have made hunting a top priority.

Trying to spend quality time afield with each of my sons while keeping a busy client schedule has never been easy. My packed calendar means the times we do spend together are even more important and always very special. For the particular year I'm going to share about, I decided to do something a bit different.

Normally I book hunters every week of hunting season, but with a huge desire to spend some of those days with my boys, I decided to reserve the entire last week of November just for us.

It was a very exhausting guide season. I basically led hunters for 10 straight weeks, spanning September to the middle of November. The guided hunts were blessed with many successes, and each of my clients was a joy to work with, but my mind and my heart continually looked forward to the special time I'd planned to spend with my sons. It seemed like forever before that special week would arrive. At last it did.

Zander, my youngest, wasn't quite ready age-wise for the kind of adventure that a remote, mountainous hunt represented. My two eldest sons, Zach and Zane, didn't officially get out of school for Thanksgiving break until Wednesday. I assumed we wouldn't get started until Thursday evening after we held our big holiday feast.

When Zane asked me to let him miss school on Monday of that week, I debated long and hard about his request. But when he added that his goal was to travel into the high country to harvest an above-average mule deer ("muley"), how could I refuse? I was an easy pushover, especially when he added that his preferred weapon of choice for the hunt would be his bow. What dad can resist taking his son hunting?

The mule deer rut season was in full swing, so the chances of finding a respectable deer seemed reasonable. We decided I would pack a rifle on my horse, and Zane would carry his compound bow in a scabbard. My interest in pulling the trigger on an animal was far outweighed by my hope that Zane would get an opportunity for a shot. With fatherly anticipation for my son's desire to be granted, we formed our strategy for the long day's hunt.

The area we were planning to hunt was about an hour drive from our ranch. We decided to take two saddle horses and a mule, the latter to help pack out the nice trophies we hoped to bag. The brisk, frosty morning began well before daylight. Zane and I easily awoke and rose from our snug, warm beds filled with eager anticipation of what might be in store for us. The horses and mule were saddled, a hearty breakfast was consumed, and lunches were packed. After traveling by pickup and trailer to a safe parking area, we quickly unloaded the animals and started up the mountain trail.

As is the case with most big-game hunting in the Western United States, being at a choice location by daylight is crucial. As you can imagine, I've spent countless hours over the years sitting atop my faithful mount while trekking up and down mountain trails in the dark. This welcome routine has come to be a very precious time of communing with my wonderful God. When I do, I'm invariably reminded of how small I really am and how awesome and gracious He is. Everything around me reminds me of His goodness.

The surefooted horse that I'm riding through the darkness, for example, makes me think of how trustworthy my Father in heaven is. The occasional glimpse of the white light of the moon and stars overhead that are set against the black night sky remind me of the light He is to this world that is sadly darkened by sin. As I ride, I can't help but praise God for His many multiplied blessings. In the quietness of the cool mountain breeze and the sound and rhythm of horse and mule hooves hitting the trail, I often find myself wiping tears from my eyes.

That morning I prayed especially for my sons. I prayed that God would help me help them know Him as I do. I thanked Him for the use of His great outdoors to reveal His majesty, creativity, strength, and love. As Zane and I rode through the predawn blackness of the timber, I felt chills of elation because the One who created this world was willing to hear the cries of my heart regarding the young men He'd placed in my care. This comforting feeling made the early-morning ride even more unforgettable.

After spending this very delightful time in the saddle, the dawning of the new day unfolded. Our eyes strained to catch even the slightest glimpse or movement of the majestic mountain monarchs we hoped would be in the area. It wasn't long before we both spotted a small buck and doe at the edge of a clearing. No sooner had we stopped our horses when Zane whispered from behind me, "Dad, I see a big buck bedded up in the timber!"

Sure enough, the buck Zane had spotted was a definite keeper. To our advantage, the handsome animal was facing away from us and hadn't detected our presence. Zane very cautiously eased off his horse, and without making even the slightest peep slid his bow out of the scabbard and began his stalk. From my position, I could see the deer and Zane. I watched as my boy closed the gap on the monster buck.

His stalk had a definite chance at being successful. Then the unexpected happened. The buck turned his head just enough for me to notice that his lower jaw had been broken and was loosely hanging down. It was a pitiful sight. Perhaps he'd gotten in a fight with another buck or was the victim of an errant rifle shot. For whatever reason, the mature mule deer had suffered such misfortune that I knew in an instant what had to be done. My heart raced as I carefully pulled my rifle from the scabbard.

It was obvious that if we didn't harvest the massive buck, his pain would continue and his inability to take in food would definitely prevent him from making it through the long winter. I decided to let Zane go ahead and arrow the animal, but if he were unsuccessful, I would follow up with a rifle shot. The plan nearly worked as Zane crept within 30 yards of the wounded muley. He stopped and as he neared full draw, the buck saw him, jumped up, and bolted away.

I wanted the deer to get a safe distance from Zane before I tried a shot, so I hollered to Zane, "That deer has a broken jaw, so I'm going to try to take him." As the deer scrambled toward heavy cover, I positioned the 7mm rifle on the last available opening through the trees that he would have to go through. Just when it entered my field of view, I squeezed the trigger. The escaping buck crumpled to the ground.

Zane joined me and said he'd also noticed the fractured jaw, so he was glad we hadn't let him get away.

We were cautious as we approached the downed animal. He had died quickly, and we were thankful that we'd helped it not suffer a slow, excruciating death. While I was disappointed that Zane wasn't the one to place his deer tag on such a large specimen, I was impressed by the maturity my son showed as he ecstatically congratulated me for downing such an awesome buck. I reminded him that the unforgettable kill was actually a product of good teamwork and gave him a well deserved "Atta boy, Zane!"

After taking the necessary time to field dress and split the carcass, we worked together to load it onto our trusty mule. We rode back to the trailhead and loaded the fine trophy into the front compartment of our horse trailer. Zane and I still had enough time to enjoy our lunch and continue our hunting adventure.

For the afternoon hunt, we decided to ride into another area, climbing to a high vantage point where we could monitor a large expanse of great muley habitat. With the rut in full swing, we hoped to locate a respectable buck and have enough daylight to carry out a stalk. A bone-chilling wind picked up as we neared the area where we planned to leave the horses and mule. As we climbed to the lookout, it was becoming difficult to glass the surrounding area due to the blowing snow. I was afraid the deer would hold tight and not show themselves.

After struggling to scan the country around us through the wintry precipitation, I located a herd of deer in a deep canyon approximately a mile away. After a closer look, much to my amazement, I noticed another great muley that appeared to be even larger than "Broken Jaw."

"Zane, I think I see another shooter!" I said excitedly as I took off my backpack and set up the spotting scope. Zane peered through the lens at the buck, and very enthusiastically affirmed my findings. I noticed that my son was breathing a little heavy as he commented on the massive set of dark-mahogany-colored antlers. It was obvious that he was stoked about giving chase to the prize below us.

Without hesitation we packed up our things, hopped on our horses, grabbed the mule's lead rope, and hurried down the mountain to close the distance as quickly as we could. We wanted to get there before the giant deer decided to move on. After tying our animals up, we scurried quietly to a location we hoped would allow us a possible shot opportunity. As we peeked over a fallen log, there lay the great buck on a ridge across from us. Three does were bedded close by.

Zane and I agreed that an archery stalk wouldn't work in this situation, and if we spooked the beast he'd probably disappear into the vast wilderness. We had plenty of time for Zane to get settled in rock solid with the 7mm. After taking careful aim and making sure he had the proper shot placement, he squeezed the trigger. His calculations were perfect! The heavy deer rolled over in his bed and permanently went to sleep.

What a precious father/son moment! We high-fived each other and headed to the downed buck. As we field dressed it and loaded it onto the mule's packsaddle, we talked about how we couldn't wait for Zack and Zander to see our trophies. While we were riding off the mountain and back to our vehicle, I reminded Zane that God had given both of us an illustration of what can happen when a man delights in the Lord. The picture came in the form of a couple of big muleys that were headed to our freezer...not to mention the sizable racks that would grace our walls, photo albums, and memories. We took a minute to stop and thank God for the bounty He'd provided. And we were sure He didn't mind us respectfully smiling large as we prayed, "Thank You, God, for the blessing of a double whammy!"

20

Dream Hunt

by Steve Chapman

People fortunate to hunt with their dads might not understand how deep the longing can be in the hearts of those who haven't experienced such a blessing. Although the following story doesn't reflect my personal experience, it does reveal what many men have shared with me over the years.

With our backs against the thick trunk of a fallen red oak tree, Dad and I quietly talked as we waited for daylight to come.

"Son," he whispered, "it's gonna be a great morning. I can feel it in my bones. Something is gonna come through this area. Before they make coffee at the diner back in town, I'm thinkin' we'll have one down and cleaned and be on our way to do some braggin' with the boys over a plate of biscuits and gravy."

I loved hearing my dad talk with me in such a confident and excited way. The flood of deer-hunting adrenaline that filled his soul was pouring over into mine. I was smiling inside and out. I was exactly where I wanted to be and where I needed to be.

Within 20 minutes the sun had once again resurrected on our side of the planet. There was plenty enough light so we could see down the ridge we were monitoring, as well as into the deep ravine we were sitting above.

Dad had used his keen understanding of whitetail behavior to pick out a travel route the local herd regularly used. There were several trails within 40 to 50 yards of where we sat that led from some nearby cornfields to one of their favorite bedding areas.

Dad was so sure we were in a "hot spot" that he reminded me to keep my gun in position so I'd be ready for a shot with the least amount of movement. I gladly followed his instructions. Several minutes ticked by without conversation. We were too busy turning our heads slowly from side to side like oscillating radar as we scanned the area for deer.

I was looking off to the left when I got a gentle nudge in my ribs from my father's elbow. He'd taught me not to snap my head around quickly when he wanted my attention because that was a type of movement easily seen by the alert eyes of deer. With a slow, deliberate motion, I turned my face toward him. Finally, in my peripheral vision, I could see his left hand resting on his leg. He was pointing to my right with his index finger.

I followed the line of sight and, sure enough, there stood a timber monster. The buck was as big as I'd ever seen in our part of the world. On first glance, I could see he sported at least 10, possibly 12 points and had gnarly drop-tines falling from his main beams.

I was sitting close enough to Dad that our camo overalls were touching. It was a closeness that was intentional on my part. I felt more connected to him when we were touching, and I'd noticed that all morning he'd never tried to pull away. Because we were so close, he could feel my body tense the moment I saw the deer. While maintaining a visual on the buck, he whispered some encouragement.

"Stay calm, son."

When I heard how tense his voice sounded, I knew the presence of such a massive rack had rattled him as much as it did me. But his experience with moments like we were facing helped him control his nerves, and, in turn, he helped me work through the heebie-jeebies.

We waited for the huge buck to drop his head and nose the leaves for some breakfast so we could take deep breaths. Once more I felt the thrill of being next to Dad and sharing such intense and enjoyable emotions. This wasn't something I stopped and thought about very often or for very long. Instead, it was an instantaneous, warm sensation that shot contentment through my soul. And knowing he wanted me beside him intensified the joy.

After what seemed to be a full-minute standoff with the cautious buck, the creature finally lowered his head and searched for acorns. Dad slowly motioned his index finger, lifting it up and down, telling me to raise my gun and get the deer in my sights. I had to shoot across his lap to take aim, and he carefully raised his knees for me to use as a rifle rest.

Moving his arms slower than the drip of honey on a cold day, he got his hands to his ears and covered them as I drew a bead on the deer's chest.

"Take 'im, son. It's now or never," he whispered.

The .30 caliber bounced on dad's knees after the shot, and a whiff of smoke drifted from the barrel. We watched as the buck ran about 30 yards, stopped, and then stood still for a few seconds. Dad and I whispered almost simultaneously, "Down! Go down!"

As if the mature buck heard our pleading, he weaved back and forth. Dad glanced over at me, showing an expression of sympathy for the mortally wounded animal. The look on his face revealed that somewhere in his hunter's heart was a soft spot. He didn't seem at all embarrassed by the feeling, and I didn't see it as a weakness. Instead, I saw his pained expression as a sign of the kind of strength I wanted to have and be comfortable enough with to show.

As the life drained from the buck's body, he stumbled to the left and then his legs went out from under him. By then we were both out of our seated positions and on our knees. It was hard to believe that such a massive deer was not just down, but it was ours to claim, to take pictures of for posterity, and to retrieve for the freezer.

Dad stood up and reminded me to put the gun safety on. Then he reached for my hand and pulled me up. He gently took my rifle and leaned it against the fallen oak. He turned to me and wrapped his big arms around me. The bear hug we were in lasted at least 10 seconds—a long time for two guys. But I didn't mind at all. We were releasing the effects of the unbridled excitement we'd felt as a team. When Dad pulled back and looked at me, I noticed tears forming in his eyes.

"You are the man, son! You are the man. Perfect morning, perfect weather, perfect spot, perfect buck, and—most important—perfect shot."

I would have to create a new language to adequately describe how happy my dad made me feel in that moment. He kept his hands on my shoulders as he continued bathing me in words of affirmation and congratulations. As he talked, I could feel something watery forming in my eyes and running down my cheeks. I wanted to fight the flow, but I figured if Dad were man enough to let it happen, I could too.

I started to say something back to Dad, but for some reason nothing would come out. I couldn't think of what to say so I just stood there looking at him, drops of salty water running down my face...

And that's when I woke up.

I'm not sure what time it was, but the blackness through my bedroom windows told me it was still nighttime. I sat up, swung my legs over the edge of the bed, and rubbed my eyes. They were damp. The darkness hid the quivering of my chin as I faced the reality that the hunting trip with my dad I'd always dreamed of was just that—a dream.

The pool of tears in my eyes got deeper the more I thought about the fact that going hunting with him was a wish that would never be filled. He'd left our family when I was five years old. The few memories I had of him only whetted my appetite to see him, hear him, touch him, and be with him again. I sat there in the unlit stillness and once more fought the anger over his longtime absence. The same questions I'd asked through the years came back to torture me. *Why would he leave us? What did I do wrong to drive him away? Did he ever love me? Why doesn't he connect with me?* And, like before, the answers never came.

I lay back down and rested my head on my pillow. I stared into the night and prayed for my dad, wherever he was. I asked God for the grace to be forgiving toward him. Then my thoughts went to the little boy who slept right above me in an upstairs bedroom. I softly whispered a promise: "Son, with God's help I'll do my best to make sure your dream hunt comes true!"

Lyric Credits

Chapter 4: The Call

1. Steve Chapman, "That's a Call," Little Dog Little Boy Music, BMI 2012. Used by permission. All rights reserved.

Chapter 10: Mountaineer Memories

1. Steve Chapman, "The Hunt Is Over," Little Dog Little Boy Music, BMI. Used by permission. All rights reserved.

Chapter 15: A Big, Ol' "Atta Dad!"

1. Steve Chapman, "Daddy's Best Sermon," Little Dog Little Boy Music, BMI. Used by permission. All rights reserved.

To the memory of Lee Gilliland—husband, father, son, brother, and member of the Harvest House team.

Lee knew firsthand the joys of hunting and the outdoors. He greatly loved the Lord, his family, and his friends.

We miss you, Lee, but we also rejoice that you are in Jesus' presence.

Steve Chapman
and
The Harvest House Family

About the Author

Steve's love of hunting began in his early teens on a weekend when one of his dad's church members invited him to tag along on an October squirrel hunt. Archery is Steve's first choice for use in the field, followed by muzzle loader, and then pistol or rifle. To date, according to Steve's calculations, he's entered the woods before daylight on more than 2000 mornings and hopes to continue that trend for many years.

Proudly claiming West Virginia as his home state, Steve grew up attending the church where his dad preached. He met his wife, Annie, in junior high school. Twelve years later they dated and then married, settling in Nashville, Tennessee. There they raised their son and daughter, Nathan and Heidi. When Nathan and Heidi both married, Steve and Annie enthusiastically accepted their new daughter-in-law and son-in-law, and now they are enjoying being grandparents.

Steve is president of S&A Family, Inc., an organization formed to oversee the production of the Chapmans' music ministries and recordings. "Family life" has been the primary theme of their lyrics since they began singing together professionally. As Dove Award-winning artists, they've performed at more than 2500 churches and recorded more than 24 albums.

Steve and Annie continue to lead marriage seminars and other workshops, write relationship and hunting books, and perform in concerts all over North America.

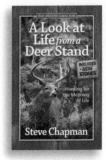

A Look at Life from a Deer Stand

From the incredible rush of bagging "the big one" to standing in awe of God's magnificent creation, Steve Chapman captures the spirit of the hunt. In short chapters filled with excitement and humor, he takes you on his successful and not-so-successful forays into the heart of deer country. As you experience the joy of scouting a trophy buck, you'll discover how the skills necessary for great hunting can help you draw closer to the Lord.

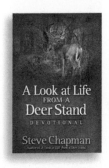

A Look at Life from a Deer Stand Devotional

Just you, God, and a whitetail. Perfect. From the moment he hits the woods to the minute he heads home, avid hunter Steve Chapman revels in the pursuit of whitetails. A vivid storyteller, he invites you to join him in the thickets, meadows, and woods to experience God's magnificent creation and discover powerful truths that reveal the awesome ways He guides you.

From the pulse-racing sight of a trophy buck to insights gleaned from a wily doe, these enthusiastic devotions will add to your hunting knowledge as you celebrate God's presence and provision.

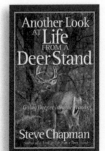

Another Look at Life from a Deer Stand

Drawing on his many years of hunting, avid sportsman Steve takes you to the forests and fields to experience the excitement of sighting whitetails and wily turkeys. From the joys of being in the woods to the thrill of handling well-made equipment, you'll relate to the adventure of going after wild game. Along the way you'll also garner some intriguing life truths that will impact your everyday life...spiritual truths that reflect the bounty and grace of the Creator.

More Great Books by Steve Chapman

10 Ways to Prepare Your Son for Life
365 Things Every Hunter Should Know
Another Look at Life from a Deer Stand
The Good Husband's Guide to Balancing Hobbies and Marriage
Great Hunting Stories
Hot Topics for Couples (with Annie Chapman)
The Hunter's Cookbook (with Annie Chapman)
A Look at Life from a Deer Stand
A Look at Life from a Deer Stand Devotional
A Look at Life from a Deer Stand Gift Edition
A Look at Life from a Deer Stand Study Guide
Stories from the Deer Stand
Wasn't It Smart of God To…
With God on a Deer Hunt

Great Books by Annie Chapman

10 Ways to Prepare Your Daughter for Life
Letting Go of Anger
The Mother-in-Law Dance
What Every Wife Wants Her Husband to Know

To read sample chapters, go to
www.HarvestHousePublishers.com

Available at your local Christian bookstore
or
www.SteveandAnnieChapman.com

Chapman Family Discography

At the Potter's House
An Evening Together
Every Moment
Family Favorites
Finish Well
For Times Like These
Gotta Get There
Hymns from God's Great Cathedral
Kiss of Hearts
Long Enough to Know
Love Was Spoken
The Miles
A Mother's Touch
Nathan Paul
Never Turn Back
The Silver Bridge
That Way Again
This House Still Stands
Tools for the Trade

To find out more about the Chapmans and their music, go to
www.SteveandAnnieChapman.com.